First paperback edition December 2021

Book design by Bare In Mind Production

ISBN 978-1-960149-00-8 (paperback)
ISBN 978-1-960149-01-5 (ebook)

www.bareinmindproductions.com

TABLE OF CONTENTS

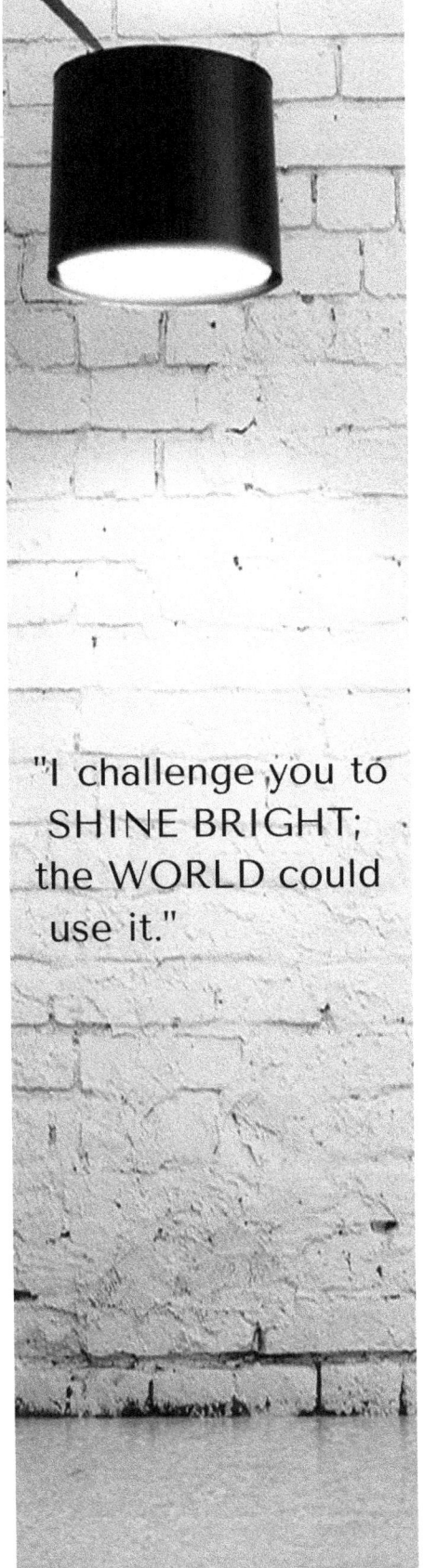

INTRODUCTION

Table of Contents 1
Words from the Author 3
Introduction 5

PLAN & PROCEDURE

Goals 7
Outcome 8
Input 9
The Plan 10
Calendar 11

EXECUTION

Execution 15
I. Planner & Journal 18
Progress Report 110
II. Planner & Journal 112
Completion Report 204

CONCLUSION

Testimony 206

"I challenge you to SHINE BRIGHT; the WORLD could use it."

I had no idea my personal journey would inspire others to challenge themselves but I am so grateful it did! Hearing all the wonderful feedback from family, friends, family of close friends or relatives to passing strangers whom decided to adapt my challenge into their daily routine inspired me to write "No Distractions, The 13 Week Challenge".

I think I can speak for everyone in the world when I say, 2020 shocked every household enforcing life changing experiences. My businesses along with the global economy was on a temporary shutdown. Fortunately, my finances allowed me to use this time to travel, reunite with my passions and even learn a few new trades. During this time, I became more hands on with my spa learning how to apply a full set of nails, makeup and individual lashes. I toured the west coast, New York, Miami and Atlanta for music. I fell in love with the piano, trading crypto and completed a book I've been working on for two years. Most importantly, I got reacquainted with God; for months it was just me and Him.

In August, I ended up having to come back home due to a very dear friend passing away. In the following four weeks I attended six more funerals. Death, always had a way of making me evaluate life and appreciate the one I have. Feeling overwhelmed with so much death in the atmosphere, I became disconnected, yearning for the peace I had while traveling.

The morning of my brother's aunt funeral, I received a call from NYC Health & Hospitals offering my former position at a higher pay for a thirteen-week contract. That evening, at a historic local bar, I was offered a bartending position as the first black bartender to ever bartend in 68 years. Honored, but truly wanting to clear my mind; unwind and drink my wine, I kindly told the owner I'll think it over. I found it odd that on the same day, two careers I previously worked and decided to leave behind came back to entice me.

I decided that I did NOT want any of those to be my options. That moment gave BIRTH to CLARITY. A fuse sparked that challenged me to experience new heights in my personal growth. I took the concept from the hospitals' contract and applied the 13 weeks to my life; achieving and seeing my goals through with no distractions. With six weeks remaining, I can tell you this challenge has changed my life. This book is proof of what DRIVE, PASSION and NO DISTRACTIONS can do. THAT'S RIGHT, I AM on this journey WITH YOU!

Keep focused and moving forward, I challenge you to SHINE BRIGHT; the WORLD could use it.

Peace and Blessings
Josefa Renee

INTRODUCTION

When we are children, we are told we can achieve anything. With this understanding, the world is filled with endless opportunities. Some of us believed we would be a famous singer practicing in the mirror. Or a teacher, giving lessons to stuffed animals in an imaginary school. That same endless imagination could quickly transfer in a second to a pretend game of being a thief in a game of cops and robbers. In these very childhood games, we were given instructions on how to develop personal strengths; some easy or difficult but to overcome and triumph. Remember the games of "SIMON SAYS"? In all of our lives there is a "SIMON" instructing us on what we should do. You were determined to become the "THE SIMON"! SO, You followed SIMON'S every move hoping to advance IN THE GAME undistracted; FOCUSED!

WHAT IF YOU intensely channeled YOUR childhood determined energy and strategically planned reinforced goals so YOUR daily affirmation was a resounding YES, I CAN? Tunnel YOUR VISION, focusing simply on YOUR goals with no distractions. As a child it may have been your parent calling you inside for dinner just before YOUR CHANCE to become leader in "RED, LIGHT, GREEN, LIGHT". Today it may be your child needing you to set aside YOUR PASSION for a steady income. Distractions come in many forms. Distractions can make necessary choices we've had to make seem hopeless and unattainable. BUT THERE IS HOPE by applying all we've learned in STRUCTURED games we played as children. So, be ENCOURAGED and lift your head up! I believe God has given us all the tools we need to turn our situation around. You didn't come this far to give up now!

No Distractions The 13 Week Challenge; shines light on goals navigating you through obvious and hidden distractions. Distractions can disable us to do what is right; the right way and at the right time. This challenge is for everyone who has planted seeds this year, five years or twenty years ago, felt rain and is wondering where is the harvest? This book will challenge you to use every Trial and Test to make you stronger. HOP SCOTCH the right steps the first time unwaveringly. Affirm, ALL THINGS are working for YOUR GOOD. YOU DIDN'T come this far to lose.

If you've purchased, made copies or borrowed this book, that is your first investment to giving your goals everything you've got, holding nothing back. I am so excited for what's ahead on your new journey equipped with ammunition to counter attack distractions - absolutely NO DISTRACTIONS!
I don't know who I'm talking to but I believe God planted this book with you and is waiting to change your story immediately. You may be in a weird place in your life and may question why certain things are not happening for you. If, we believe that the world was created in 7 days; just imagine what can happen in 13 weeks. I challenge you, NO MORE excuses or DISTRACTIONS.

Get in and WIN the GAME; I DOUBLE DARE YOU!!

GOALS

LIST IN PRIORITY YOUR GOALS. ONE BEING THE MAIN, WHETHER PERSONAL, FINANCIAL OR EMOTIONAL. ANY FIVE GOALS YOU CHOOSE, JOT THEM DOWN

EXAMPLE

1. Lose weight for Jason's weddings
2. Buy a new car
3. Repair relationship with sister
4. Find a new career
5. Complete projects for home, work and committee

GOALS

Meditate on your list with a clear understanding of the task ahead. Do any of your goals work together?

OUTCOME

I FIND THAT KNOWING THE OUTCOME, WORKING BACKWARDS AND UNDOING THE PROCESS IN REVERSE, MAKES PLANNING YOUR APPROACH EASIER IN ACCOMPLISHING GOALS. IN THIS SECTION, FOR EACH GOAL, FILL IN REASONABLE EXPECTATIONS AND SELECT A DUE DATE. THE DEADLINE DOES NOT HAVE TO BE WITHIN THE 13 WEEKS CHALLENGE.

Lose 50LBS Fit Size 8	Purchase 2020 MAZDA CX-5	Find a new career	Repair relationship w. Kayden	Complete - projects for home, work & committee
Summer 2023	February 10, 2023	Spring 2024	April 3, 2023	March 2, 2023

DUE:

DUE:

DUE:

DUE:

DUE:

NOTES:

_____

_____

_____

_____

_____

INPUT

NOW, THAT YOU KNOW EXACTLY WHAT YOU WANT, IT'S TIME TO FOCUS ON WHAT REQUIREMENTS YOU NEED TO MEET THESE EXPECTATIONS. FOR EACH OUTCOME, FILL IN REASONABLE EXPECTATIONS AND LIST REASONS YOU STRUGGLE IN THIS AREA.

DIFFICULTIES				
Unmotivated & don't have time	Low funds & credit score	I don't know where to begin	I don't know her number	I don't have time
Lose 50LBS Fit Size 8	Purchase 2020 MAZDA CX-5	A Career doing what I love	Repair relationship w. Kayden	Complete: projects for home, work & committee

DIFFICULTIES

DIFFICULTIES

DIFFICULTIES

DIFFICULTIES

DIFFICULTIES

DIFFICULTIES

NOTES:

_____

_____

_____

_____

THE PLAN

WITHOUT A PLAN YOU WILL FIND YOURSELF SLIPPING INTO INEFFECTIVE ACTIONS OR WASTED TIME. PLANNING MAKES KNOWING WHEN AND HOW TO EXECUTE EASIER! FOR EACH GOAL, JOT DOWN, A STEP-BY- STEP PLAN TO SEE PROGRESS IN THAT AREA.

Lose 3 lbs a week

Lose 50LBS by Summer

Repair my credit; earn extra money

Purchase Car by February

Narrow down my interest & passions

New Career by Spring

Search Kayden's Facebook

Rebuild w. sister by April 3rd

Use 24hrs wisely. 8hrs Sleep, 8hrs work (complete 1 contract every week), 2hrs time for myself, 1hr dedicated to renovating bathroom and 1hr planning fundraiser.

Finalize 8 contracts, Plan Fund Raiser & Renovate Bathroom by March 2nd

NOTES:

_____

_____

_____

_____

CALENDAR

"You automatically lose the chances you don't take."

MONTH

S	M	T	W	T	F	S

NOTES:

CALENDAR

"You automatically lose the chances you don't take."

MONTH

S	M	T	W	T	F	S

NOTES:

_____

_____

_____

_____

CALENDAR

"You automatically lose the chances you don't take."

MONTH

S	M	T	W	T	F	S

NOTES:

EXECUTION

LET'S IMAGINE OURSELVES CRUISING INTO OUR DAY. WE JUST HOPPED INTO OUR
VEHICLE BUT IN ORDER TO GET TO OUR DESTINATION, THERE ARE THINGS WE NEED.
WITHOUT THE RIGHT EQUIPMENT, LIKE THE KEYS AND FUEL, WE COULDN'T GO ANYWHERE. I RECOMMEND STARTING YOUR DAILY ENGINE WITH POSITIVITY.

BEGIN EVERY DAY WITH A CLEAR MIND AND HEART!

BEFORE TURNING THE TELEVISION ON, READING TEXT MESSAGES, ANSWERING EMAILS
OR CHECKING INSTAGRAM TAKE 5-10 MINUTES TO CLEAR YOUR THOUGHTS AND PROJECT YOUR ENERGY FOR THE DAY.

NEXT, LIST YOUR TASK(S) FOCUSING ON WHAT YOU CAN ACCOMPLISH THAT PARTICULAR DAY TOWARDS YOUR GOALS.

LAST, LOOK BACK AT YOUR DAY. KEEP A JOURNAL AND DOCUMENT DISTRACTIONS YOU RECOGNIZE THROUGHOUT THE DAY. THIS JOURNEY IS ABOUT AVOIDING ANYTHING THAT TAKES YOUR ATTENTION AWAY FROM YOUR GOALS AND FOCUSES SOLELY ON THE ROAD AHEAD.

IF, YOU AREN'T SURE IF YOUR FOCUS IS BEING DISTRACTED, ASK YOURSELF, "WHAT DOES THIS SITUATION HAVE TO DO WITH THE GOALS ON MY LIST?"

EYES HAVEN'T SEEN, EARS HAVEN'T HEARD, THE BLESSINGS GOD HAS PREPARED FOR YOU. THE GOD WHO CREATED THE UNIVERSE IS EAGER TO SPEND TIME WITH YOU. TALK TO YOUR CREATOR! RELY ON HIM TO HELP YOU BE STRONG THROUGHOUT THIS CHALLENGE AND TO GUIDE YOU TO YOUR PURPOSE. IF AT ANY TIME THROUGHOUT THE DAY, YOUR ENGINE IS RUNNING LOW, GAS UP WITH PRAYER AND WORDS OF MOTIVATION; IT'S FREE!

LET'S GO!

First Quarter

Day 1-23 / 3 Weeks

Second Quarter

Day 23-46 / 6-7 Weeks

Third Quarter

Day 46-69 / 7-10 Weeks

Fourth Quarter

Day 69-91 / 10-13 Weeks

PRODUCTIVITY PLANNER

SAMPLE

DAILY PRAYER

If and when I feel doubtful, anxious, impatient, unmotivated, or overwhelmed, God remind me that You are above all things and You hold all things together. Lead me to my purpose. Amen

DAILY REFLECTION

Now to him who is able to do immeasurably more than all we ask or imagine, according to his power that is at work within us , - Ephesians 3:20

WAKE TIME

8:00 AM

SCHEDULE

8:00	**PRAYER, MANTRA & PLAN DAY**
9:00	**TAKE ALEX TO SCHOOL**
10:00	**PICK UP GROCERIES**
11:00	**EMAIL CONTRACTS TO CLIENTS**
12:00	**RESEARCH FUNDRAISER IDEAS**
13:00	**CONTACT CREDITOR**
14:00	**WALK TO DELI FOR SALAD**
15:00	**LOOK FOR KAYDEN'S CONTACT**
16:00	**SELF CARE**
17:00	**PICK UP ALEX**
18:00	**HELP ALEX WITH HOMEWORK**
19:00	**FIX DINNER & PREP MEALS**
20:00	**SELF CARE**
21:00	**PUT ALEX TO BED**
22:00	**CLEAN BATHROOM**
23:00	**SHOWER & GO TO BED**

TODAY'S MANTRA

GET FOCUSED

TOP PRIORITIES

- [ ] **EXERCISE 20-30 MINS**
- [ ] **GET IN CONTACT WITH KAYDEN**
- [ ] **PLAN FUNDRAISER**

TO-DO LIST

- [ ] 1. EAT A LIGHT LUNCH AND TAKE A 20 MIN WALK DURING MY BREAK
- [ ] 2. CONTACT A CREDIT REPAIR CONSULTANT
- [ ] 3. GIVE ALL 8 CLIENTS A DEADLINE TO HAVE CONTRACTS COMPLETED 2 WEEKS BEFORE THE ACTUAL DEADLINE
- [ ] 4. SPEND 30 MINS SEARCHING MY EMAILS & FACEBOOK FOR KAY'S CONTACT INFO
- [ ] 5. SPEND 20-40 MINS ASKING PEOPLE AND RESEARCHING EASY, EFFICIENT FUNDRAISER IDEAS
- [ ] 6. PICK UP GROCERIES TO PREPARE MEALS AT HOME
- [ ] 7. HELP ALEX WITH HIS HOMEWORK 8. 10-15 MINS BEFORE I SHOWER, CLEAN THE BATHROOM
- [ ] _____
- [ ] _____
- [ ] _____

REFLECTION JOURNAL

SAMPLE

First Quarter
Day 1-23 / 3 Weeks

Second Quarter
Day 23-46 / 6-7 Weeks

Third Quarter
Day 46-69 / 7-10 Weeks

Fourth Quarter
Day 69-91 / 10-13 Weeks

Today's Distractions
-Neighbor asked me to dog-sit for 2 weeks w/o pay
-Carlos from HR called me complaining about management
-Alex wrote on the walls with a crayon
-Played Candy Crush for 40 minutes
-Surfed Instagram for 1 hour

Today I

woke up feeling hopeful for this challenge and excited for my goals. Right up until, I saw Alex's painting on my living room wall. My mother is coming by this weekend and I barely have time to manage life and get the house in order. Alex's painting of us was sweet. It made me smile but I ended up cleaning his artwork instead of the bathroom. Lauren asked me to watch her Yorkie while she's on vacation. He's actually a good dog but this is not on my **No Distractions list**. She's not paying to dog-sit and it will take time away from my daily tasks. I realized I spent 40 minutes today playing Candy Crush and 1 hour on Instagram. I should've used that time for planning the fundraiser and contacting a credit consultant. I was productive in finding Kayden's Facebook account. Also, I informed all my clients to have all of their paperwork in within 30 days for contracts to be finalized. While walking on my lunch break, I noticed a salsa class. Tomorrow, I'll inquire about classes. I plan to wake up an hour earlier to clean the bathroom and research fundraiser ideas.

PRODUCTIVITY PLANNER

DAILY PRAYER

As I begin this challenge, I pray that I would confidently pursue the things that God has crafted me to do. When I am feeling discouraged, worried, frustrated or overwhelmed. Help me to immerse myself in your light. Your encouraging words can pierce through darkness. Amen

DAILY REFLECTION

Hebrews 4:12 NIV
For the word of God is alive and active. Sharper than any double-edged sword, it penetrates even to dividing soul and spirit, joints and marrow; it judges the thoughts and attitudes of the heart.

WAKE TIME

_____

TODAY'S MANTRA

_____

SCHEDULE

8:00	_____
9:00	_____
10:00	_____
11:00	_____
12:00	_____
13:00	_____
14:00	_____
15:00	_____
16:00	_____
17:00	_____
18:00	_____
19:00	_____
20:00	_____
21:00	_____
22:00	_____
23:00	_____

TOP PRIORITIES

- ☐ _____
- ☐ _____
- ☐ _____

TO-DO LIST

- ☐ _____
- ☐ _____
- ☐ _____
- ☐ _____
- ☐ _____
- ☐ _____
- ☐ _____
- ☐ _____
- ☐ _____
- ☐ _____
- ☐ _____

REFLECTION JOURNAL

DATE _____

First Quarter
Day 1-23 / 3 Weeks

Second Quarter
Day 23-46 / 6-7 Weeks

Third Quarter
Day 46-69 / 7-10 Weeks

Fourth Quarter
Day 69-91 / 10-13 Weeks

Today's Distractions

Today I

_____

_____

_____

_____

_____

_____

_____

_____

PRODUCTIVITY PLANNER

DAILY PRAYER

Today I pray against every distraction that comes in the way of my success. Teach me to identify distractions when I come across one. Amen

DAILY REFLECTION

1 Corinthians 10:13 NIV
No temptation has overtaken you except what is common to mankind. And God is faithful; he will not let you be tempted beyond what you can bear. But when you are tempted, he will also provide a way out so that you can endure it.

WAKE TIME

_____

TODAY'S MANTRA

_____

SCHEDULE

8:00 _____

9:00 _____

10:00 _____

11:00 _____

12:00 _____

13:00 _____

14:00 _____

15:00 _____

16:00 _____

17:00 _____

18:00 _____

19:00 _____

20:00 _____

21:00 _____

22:00 _____

23:00 _____

TOP PRIORITIES

- [ ] _____
- [ ] _____
- [ ] _____

TO-DO LIST

- [ ] _____
- [ ] _____
- [ ] _____
- [ ] _____
- [ ] _____
- [ ] _____
- [ ] _____
- [ ] _____
- [ ] _____
- [ ] _____
- [ ] _____
- [ ] _____

REFLECTION JOURNAL

DATE _____

First Quarter
Day 1-23 / 3 Weeks

Second Quarter
Day 23-46 / 6-7 Weeks

Third Quarter
Day 46-69 / 7-10 Weeks

Fourth Quarter
Day 69-91 / 10-13 Weeks

Today's Distractions

Today I

_____

_____

_____

_____

_____

_____

_____

_____

PRODUCTIVITY PLANNER

DAILY PRAYER

I'm grateful for waking up today. I'm grateful for my health and the ability to function in life on my own. Amen

DAILY REFLECTION

John 15:16 NIV
You did not choose me, but I chose you and appointed you so that you might go and bear fruit—fruit that will last—and so that whatever you ask in my name the Father will give you.

WAKE TIME

TODAY'S MANTRA

_____

SCHEDULE

8:00	_____
9:00	_____
10:00	_____
11:00	_____
12:00	_____
13:00	_____
14:00	_____
15:00	_____
16:00	_____
17:00	_____
18:00	_____
19:00	_____
20:00	_____
21:00	_____
22:00	_____
23:00	_____

TOP PRIORITIES

- [ ] _____
- [ ] _____
- [ ] _____

TO-DO LIST

- [ ] _____
- [ ] _____
- [ ] _____
- [ ] _____
- [ ] _____
- [ ] _____
- [ ] _____
- [ ] _____
- [ ] _____
- [ ] _____
- [ ] _____
- [ ] _____

REFLECTION JOURNAL

First Quarter
Day 1-23 / 3 Weeks

Second Quarter
Day 23-46 / 6-7 Weeks

Third Quarter
Day 46-69 / 7-10 Weeks

Fourth Quarter
Day 69-91 / 10-13 Weeks

Today's Distractions

Today I

_____

_____

_____

_____

_____

_____

_____

_____

PRODUCTIVITY PLANNER

DAILY PRAYER

When people let me down, break my heart or let me fall, I give all my concerns to You. You have, provided for me before.
I need You to do it again. Amen

DAILY REFLECTION

Mark 11:24 NIV
Therefore, I tell you, whatever you ask for in prayer, believe that you have received it, and it will be yours.

WAKE TIME

_____

TODAY'S MANTRA

_____

SCHEDULE

8:00 _____
9:00 _____
10:00 _____
11:00 _____
12:00 _____
13:00 _____
14:00 _____
15:00 _____
16:00 _____
17:00 _____
18:00 _____
19:00 _____
20:00 _____
21:00 _____
22:00 _____
23:00 _____

TOP PRIORITIES

☐ _____
☐ _____
☐ _____

TO-DO LIST

☐ _____
☐ _____
☐ _____
☐ _____
☐ _____
☐ _____
☐ _____
☐ _____
☐ _____
☐ _____
☐ _____

REFLECTION JOURNAL

First Quarter
Day 1-23 / 3 Weeks

Second Quarter
Day 23-46 / 6-7 Weeks

Third Quarter
Day 46-69 / 7-10 Weeks

Fourth Quarter
Day 69-91 / 10-13 Weeks

Today's Distractions

Today I

_____

_____

_____

_____

_____

_____

_____

_____

PRODUCTIVITY PLANNER

DATE _____

DAILY PRAYER

When I do good, people want to see the worst in me. I don't want it to be this way. You see the best in me. Help me to be encouraged and heal my heart. Take away my pain. Everything that can hold me back, I ask that You take it away. I will be the best version of myself. Amen

DAILY REFLECTION

James 1:3 NIV
because you know that the testing of your faith produces perseverance.

WAKE TIME

_____

TODAY'S MANTRA

_____

SCHEDULE

8:00 _____
9:00 _____
10:00 _____
11:00 _____
12:00 _____
13:00 _____
14:00 _____
15:00 _____
16:00 _____
17:00 _____
18:00 _____
19:00 _____
20:00 _____
21:00 _____
22:00 _____
23:00 _____

TOP PRIORITIES

☐ _____
☐ _____
☐ _____

TO-DO LIST

☐ _____
☐ _____
☐ _____
☐ _____
☐ _____
☐ _____
☐ _____
☐ _____
☐ _____
☐ _____
☐ _____

REFLECTION JOURNAL

First Quarter
Day 1-23 / 3 Weeks

Second Quarter
Day 23-46 / 6-7 Weeks

Third Quarter
Day 46-69 / 7-10 Weeks

Fourth Quarter
Day 69-91 / 10-13 Weeks

Today's Distractions

Today I

_____

_____

_____

_____

_____

_____

_____

_____

PRODUCTIVITY PLANNER

DAILY PRAYER

You see my heart and know my intentions. There is nothing that compares to Your presence and companionship. Thank You for Your genuine support and friendship. Amen

DAILY REFLECTION

James 1:4 NIV
Let perseverance finish its work so that you may be mature and complete, not lacking anything.

WAKE TIME

_____

TODAY'S MANTRA

_____

SCHEDULE

8:00	_____
9:00	_____
10:00	_____
11:00	_____
12:00	_____
13:00	_____
14:00	_____
15:00	_____
16:00	_____
17:00	_____
18:00	_____
19:00	_____
20:00	_____
21:00	_____
22:00	_____
23:00	_____

TOP PRIORITIES

☐ _____
☐ _____
☐ _____

TO-DO LIST

☐ _____
☐ _____
☐ _____
☐ _____
☐ _____
☐ _____
☐ _____
☐ _____
☐ _____
☐ _____
☐ _____
☐ _____

REFLECTION JOURNAL

First Quarter
Day 1-23 / 3 Weeks

Second Quarter
Day 23-46 / 6-7 Weeks

Third Quarter
Day 46-69 / 7-10 Weeks

Fourth Quarter
Day 69-91 / 10-13 Weeks

Today's Distractions

Today I

_____

_____

_____

_____

_____

_____

_____

_____

PRODUCTIVITY PLANNER

DAILY PRAYER

Life can be so distracting. God, remind
me that everything else can wait.
If I put You first, You said You would
supply my every need. Amen

DAILY REFLECTION

James 1:5 NIV
If any of you lacks wisdom, you should ask
God, who gives generously to all without
finding fault, and it will be given to you.

WAKE TIME

TODAY'S MANTRA

_____

SCHEDULE

8:00 _____

9:00 _____

10:00 _____

11:00 _____

12:00 _____

13:00 _____

14:00 _____

15:00 _____

16:00 _____

17:00 _____

18:00 _____

19:00 _____

20:00 _____

21:00 _____

22:00 _____

23:00 _____

TOP PRIORITIES

☐ _____

☐ _____

☐ _____

TO-DO LIST

☐ _____

☐ _____

☐ _____

☐ _____

☐ _____

☐ _____

☐ _____

☐ _____

☐ _____

☐ _____

☐ _____

REFLECTION JOURNAL

DATE _____

First Quarter
Day 1-23 / 3 Weeks

Second Quarter
Day 23-46 / 6-7 Weeks

Third Quarter
Day 46-69 / 7-10 Weeks

Fourth Quarter
Day 69-91 / 10-13 Weeks

Today's Distractions

Today I

_____

_____

_____

_____

_____

_____

_____

_____

PRODUCTIVITY PLANNER

DAILY PRAYER

It seems like the devil is hitting me with everything
he can find but I believe,
You will come through. I give you praise
from deep within my soul. You are
trustworthy, patient and gracious. I
believe You can transform my situation.
Amen

DAILY REFLECTION

James 1:6 NIV
But when you ask, you must believe and
not doubt, because the one who doubts
is like a wave of the sea, blown and
tossed by the wind.

WAKE TIME

TODAY'S MANTRA

SCHEDULE

8:00 _____

9:00 _____

10:00 _____

11:00 _____

12:00 _____

13:00 _____

14:00 _____

15:00 _____

16:00 _____

17:00 _____

18:00 _____

19:00 _____

20:00 _____

21:00 _____

22:00 _____

23:00 _____

TOP PRIORITIES

☐ _____

☐ _____

☐ _____

TO-DO LIST

☐ _____

☐ _____

☐ _____

☐ _____

☐ _____

☐ _____

☐ _____

☐ _____

☐ _____

☐ _____

☐ _____

☐ _____

REFLECTION JOURNAL

First Quarter
Day 1-23 / 3 Weeks

Second Quarter
Day 23-46 / 6-7 Weeks

Third Quarter
Day 46-69 / 7-10 Weeks

Fourth Quarter
Day 69-91 / 10-13 Weeks

Today's Distractions

Today I

_____

_____

_____

_____

_____

_____

_____

_____

PRODUCTIVITY PLANNER

DATE _____

DAILY PRAYER

My past is over, today I'm not going back.
I'm excited for my future. Prepare me
mentally, physically, financially for every blessing.
Amen

DAILY REFLECTION

2 Corinthians 5:5 NIV
Now the one who has fashioned us for this
very purpose is God, who has given us the
Spirit as a deposit, guaranteeing what is to
come.

WAKE TIME

_____

TODAY'S MANTRA

_____

SCHEDULE

8:00 _____
9:00 _____
10:00 _____
11:00 _____
12:00 _____
13:00 _____
14:00 _____
15:00 _____
16:00 _____
17:00 _____
18:00 _____
19:00 _____
20:00 _____
21:00 _____
22:00 _____
23:00 _____

TOP PRIORITIES

☐ _____
☐ _____
☐ _____

TO-DO LIST

☐ _____
☐ _____
☐ _____
☐ _____
☐ _____
☐ _____
☐ _____
☐ _____
☐ _____
☐ _____
☐ _____
☐ _____

REFLECTION JOURNAL

DATE _____

First Quarter
Day 1-23 / 3 Weeks

Second Quarter
Day 23-46 / 6-7 Weeks

Third Quarter
Day 46-69 / 7-10 Weeks

Fourth Quarter
Day 69-91 / 10-13 Weeks

Today's Distractions

Today I

_____

_____

_____

_____

_____

_____

_____

_____

PRODUCTIVITY PLANNER

DATE _____

DAILY PRAYER

I've been doing everything all on my own.
Help me to not give up but to give
You all my cares and concerns. Show
me what to do. I realize I can't do it
without You. I give You my heart and
mind, take control. Amen

DAILY REFLECTION

2 Corinthians 5:7 NIV
For we live by faith, not by sight.

WAKE TIME

_____

TODAY'S MANTRA

_____

SCHEDULE

8:00 _____
9:00 _____
10:00 _____
11:00 _____
12:00 _____
13:00 _____
14:00 _____
15:00 _____
16:00 _____
17:00 _____
18:00 _____
19:00 _____
20:00 _____
21:00 _____
22:00 _____
23:00 _____

TOP PRIORITIES

- [ ] _____
- [ ] _____
- [ ] _____

TO-DO LIST

- [ ] _____
- [ ] _____
- [ ] _____
- [ ] _____
- [ ] _____
- [ ] _____
- [ ] _____
- [ ] _____
- [ ] _____
- [ ] _____
- [ ] _____
- [ ] _____

REFLECTION JOURNAL

DATE _____

First Quarter
Day 1-23 / 3 Weeks

Second Quarter
Day 23-46 / 6-7 Weeks

Third Quarter
Day 46-69 / 7-10 Weeks

Fourth Quarter
Day 69-91 / 10-13 Weeks

Today's Distractions

Today I

_____

_____

_____

_____

_____

_____

_____

_____

_____

PRODUCTIVITY PLANNER

DATE _____

DAILY PRAYER

Where would I be without You. You are
just a prayer away. I am so glad
You walk with me and guide my steps.
Lead me into a life filled with purpose
Amen

DAILY REFLECTION

Galatians 6:9 NIV
Let us not become weary in doing good,
for at the proper time we will reap a
harvest if we do not give up.

WAKE TIME

TODAY'S MANTRA

_____

SCHEDULE

8:00	_____
9:00	_____
10:00	_____
11:00	_____
12:00	_____
13:00	_____
14:00	_____
15:00	_____
16:00	_____
17:00	_____
18:00	_____
19:00	_____
20:00	_____
21:00	_____
22:00	_____
23:00	_____

TOP PRIORITIES

- ☐ _____
- ☐ _____
- ☐ _____

TO-DO LIST

- ☐ _____
- ☐ _____
- ☐ _____
- ☐ _____
- ☐ _____
- ☐ _____
- ☐ _____
- ☐ _____
- ☐ _____
- ☐ _____
- ☐ _____
- ☐ _____

REFLECTION JOURNAL

First Quarter
Day 1-23 / 3 Weeks

Second Quarter
Day 23-46 / 6-7 Weeks

Third Quarter
Day 46-69 / 7-10 Weeks

Fourth Quarter
Day 69-91 / 10-13 Weeks

Today's Distractions

Today I

_____

_____

_____

_____

_____

_____

_____

_____

PRODUCTIVITY PLANNER

DAILY PRAYER

My life is not my own. I didn't wake myself
up nor did I provide the air I breathe.
Take my life and use it as Your example,
to fulfill Your purpose. Amen

DAILY REFLECTION

Galatians 6:8 NIV
Whoever sows to please their flesh, from
the flesh will reap destruction;
whoever sows to please the
Spirit, from the Spirit will reap eternal life.

WAKE TIME

_____

TODAY'S MANTRA

_____

SCHEDULE

8:00	_____
9:00	_____
10:00	_____
11:00	_____
12:00	_____
13:00	_____
14:00	_____
15:00	_____
16:00	_____
17:00	_____
18:00	_____
19:00	_____
20:00	_____
21:00	_____
22:00	_____
23:00	_____

TOP PRIORITIES

- ☐ _____
- ☐ _____
- ☐ _____

TO-DO LIST

- ☐ _____
- ☐ _____
- ☐ _____
- ☐ _____
- ☐ _____
- ☐ _____
- ☐ _____
- ☐ _____
- ☐ _____
- ☐ _____
- ☐ _____

REFLECTION JOURNAL

DATE _____

First Quarter
Day 1-23 / 3 Weeks

Second Quarter
Day 23-46 / 6-7 Weeks

Third Quarter
Day 46-69 / 7-10 Weeks

Fourth Quarter
Day 69-91 / 10-13 Weeks

Today's Distractions

Today I

_____

_____

_____

_____

_____

_____

_____

_____

PRODUCTIVITY PLANNER

DAILY PRAYER

Sometimes I fall but I'm so grateful that You pick me up. Thank You for my life, my health and being my strength.
Amen

DAILY REFLECTION

Galatians 6:10 NIV
Therefore, as we have opportunity, let us do good to all people, especially to those who belong to the family of believers.

WAKE TIME

_____

TODAY'S MANTRA

_____

SCHEDULE

8:00 _____
9:00 _____
10:00 _____
11:00 _____
12:00 _____
13:00 _____
14:00 _____
15:00 _____
16:00 _____
17:00 _____
18:00 _____
19:00 _____
20:00 _____
21:00 _____
22:00 _____
23:00 _____

TOP PRIORITIES

☐ _____
☐ _____
☐ _____

TO-DO LIST

☐ _____
☐ _____
☐ _____
☐ _____
☐ _____
☐ _____
☐ _____
☐ _____
☐ _____
☐ _____
☐ _____

REFLECTION JOURNAL

DATE _____

First Quarter
Day 1-23 / 3 Weeks

Second Quarter
Day 23-46 / 6-7 Weeks

Third Quarter
Day 46-69 / 7-10 Weeks

Fourth Quarter
Day 69-91 / 10-13 Weeks

Today's Distractions

Today I

_____

_____

_____

_____

_____

_____

_____

_____

PRODUCTIVITY PLANNER

DAILY PRAYER

My heart wants to do right, show me what I need to do. When I think back on things You have done for me I can't help but thank You. You've brought me out of some rough times when I thought all hope was gone. I'm so glad You didn't give up on me. Continue to take control. I want more for my life. Amen

DAILY REFLECTION

Galatians 5:23 NIV
gentleness and self-control.
Against such things there is no law.

WAKE TIME

_____

TODAY'S MANTRA

_____

SCHEDULE

8:00	_____
9:00	_____
10:00	_____
11:00	_____
12:00	_____
13:00	_____
14:00	_____
15:00	_____
16:00	_____
17:00	_____
18:00	_____
19:00	_____
20:00	_____
21:00	_____
22:00	_____
23:00	_____

TOP PRIORITIES

☐ _____
☐ _____
☐ _____

TO-DO LIST

☐ _____
☐ _____
☐ _____
☐ _____
☐ _____
☐ _____
☐ _____
☐ _____
☐ _____
☐ _____
☐ _____
☐ _____

REFLECTION JOURNAL

First Quarter
Day 1-23 / 3 Weeks

Second Quarter
Day 23-46 / 6-7 Weeks

Third Quarter
Day 46-69 / 7-10 Weeks

Fourth Quarter
Day 69-91 / 10-13 Weeks

Today's Distractions

Today I

_____

_____

_____

_____

_____

_____

_____

_____

PRODUCTIVITY PLANNER

DAILY PRAYER

Today I pray for endurance and strength.
I've made up in my mind, today I will win. Amen

DAILY REFLECTION

Isaiah 6:8 NIV
Then I heard the voice of the Lord saying,
"Whom shall I send?
And who will go for us?"
And I said, "Here am I. Send me!"

WAKE TIME

_____

TODAY'S MANTRA

_____

SCHEDULE

8:00 _____
9:00 _____
10:00 _____
11:00 _____
12:00 _____
13:00 _____
14:00 _____
15:00 _____
16:00 _____
17:00 _____
18:00 _____
19:00 _____
20:00 _____
21:00 _____
22:00 _____
23:00 _____

TOP PRIORITIES

☐ _____
☐ _____
☐ _____

TO-DO LIST

☐ _____
☐ _____
☐ _____
☐ _____
☐ _____
☐ _____
☐ _____
☐ _____
☐ _____
☐ _____
☐ _____

REFLECTION JOURNAL

First Quarter
Day 1-23 / 3 Weeks

Second Quarter
Day 23-46 / 6-7 Weeks

Third Quarter
Day 46-69 / 7-10 Weeks

Fourth Quarter
Day 69-91 / 10-13 Weeks

Today's Distractions

Today I

_____

_____

_____

_____

_____

_____

_____

_____

_____

PRODUCTIVITY PLANNER

DATE _____

DAILY PRAYER

If at any time I feel hopeless and confused;
Or, like nobody understands. Help me to
be encouraged and keep faith in the seeds
I am sowing. Amen

DAILY REFLECTION

Jeremiah 32:27 NIV
"I am the LORD, the God of all mankind. Is
anything too hard for me?

WAKE TIME

_____

TODAY'S MANTRA

_____

SCHEDULE

8:00	_____
9:00	_____
10:00	_____
11:00	_____
12:00	_____
13:00	_____
14:00	_____
15:00	_____
16:00	_____
17:00	_____
18:00	_____
19:00	_____
20:00	_____
21:00	_____
22:00	_____
23:00	_____

TOP PRIORITIES

☐ _____
☐ _____
☐ _____

TO-DO LIST

☐ _____
☐ _____
☐ _____
☐ _____
☐ _____
☐ _____
☐ _____
☐ _____
☐ _____
☐ _____
☐ _____
☐ _____

REFLECTION JOURNAL

DATE _____

First Quarter
Day 1-23 / 3 Weeks

Second Quarter
Day 23-46 / 6-7 Weeks

Third Quarter
Day 46-69 / 7-10 Weeks

Fourth Quarter
Day 69-91 / 10-13 Weeks

Today's Distractions

Today I

_____

_____

_____

_____

_____

_____

_____

_____

PRODUCTIVITY PLANNER

DAILY PRAYER

If I feel like nobody cares. I know that
You care and will be my side. Amen

DAILY REFLECTION

Jeremiah 29:11 NIV
For I know the plans I have for you,"
declares the LORD, "plans to prosper
you and not to harm you, plans to give
you hope and a future.

WAKE TIME

_____

TODAY'S MANTRA

_____

SCHEDULE

8:00 _____

9:00 _____

10:00 _____

11:00 _____

12:00 _____

13:00 _____

14:00 _____

15:00 _____

16:00 _____

17:00 _____

18:00 _____

19:00 _____

20:00 _____

21:00 _____

22:00 _____

23:00 _____

TOP PRIORITIES

- [ ] _____
- [ ] _____
- [ ] _____

TO-DO LIST

- [ ] _____
- [ ] _____
- [ ] _____
- [ ] _____
- [ ] _____
- [ ] _____
- [ ] _____
- [ ] _____
- [ ] _____
- [ ] _____
- [ ] _____
- [ ] _____

REFLECTION JOURNAL

First Quarter
Day 1-23 / 3 Weeks

Second Quarter
Day 23-46 / 6-7 Weeks

Third Quarter
Day 46-69 / 7-10 Weeks

Fourth Quarter
Day 69-91 / 10-13 Weeks

Today's Distractions

Today I

_____

_____

_____

_____

_____

_____

_____

_____

_____

PRODUCTIVITY PLANNER

DATE _____

DAILY PRAYER

I want to multiply my productivity and all
that I am. I know there is so much more
that You require of me. Guide my steps,
show me when to move and when to wait. Amen

DAILY REFLECTION

James 1:20 NIV
because human anger does not
produce the righteousness that
God desires.

WAKE TIME

_____

TODAY'S MANTRA

_____

SCHEDULE

8:00 _____
9:00 _____
10:00 _____
11:00 _____
12:00 _____
13:00 _____
14:00 _____
15:00 _____
16:00 _____
17:00 _____
18:00 _____
19:00 _____
20:00 _____
21:00 _____
22:00 _____
23:00 _____

TOP PRIORITIES

- [ ] _____
- [ ] _____
- [ ] _____

TO-DO LIST

- [ ] _____
- [ ] _____
- [ ] _____
- [ ] _____
- [ ] _____
- [ ] _____
- [ ] _____
- [ ] _____
- [ ] _____
- [ ] _____
- [ ] _____
- [ ] _____

REFLECTION JOURNAL

First Quarter
Day 1-23 / 3 Weeks

Second Quarter
Day 23-46 / 6-7 Weeks

Third Quarter
Day 46-69 / 7-10 Weeks

Fourth Quarter
Day 69-91 / 10-13 Weeks

Today's Distractions

Today I

_____

_____

_____

_____

_____

_____

_____

_____

PRODUCTIVITY PLANNER

DATE _____

DAILY PRAYER

Help me to be generous and patient.
When I think of Your goodness to me,
You are loving and kind. Make me more
like You. Amen

DAILY REFLECTION

James 1:17 NIV
Every good and perfect gift is from above,
coming down from the Father of the
heavenly lights, who does not change like
shifting shadows.

WAKE TIME

_____

TODAY'S MANTRA

_____

SCHEDULE

8:00	_____
9:00	_____
10:00	_____
11:00	_____
12:00	_____
13:00	_____
14:00	_____
15:00	_____
16:00	_____
17:00	_____
18:00	_____
19:00	_____
20:00	_____
21:00	_____
22:00	_____
23:00	_____

TOP PRIORITIES

☐ _____
☐ _____
☐ _____

TO-DO LIST

☐ _____
☐ _____
☐ _____
☐ _____
☐ _____
☐ _____
☐ _____
☐ _____
☐ _____
☐ _____
☐ _____
☐ _____

REFLECTION JOURNAL

DATE _____

First Quarter
Day 1-23 / 3 Weeks

Second Quarter
Day 23-46 / 6-7 Weeks

Third Quarter
Day 46-69 / 7-10 Weeks

Fourth Quarter
Day 69-91 / 10-13 Weeks

Today's Distractions

Today I

_____

_____

_____

_____

_____

_____

_____

_____

_____

PRODUCTIVITY PLANNER

DATE _____

DAILY PRAYER

I am not the same. I am changing for
the better. Help me to be a better person,
understanding and patient with people.
Amen

DAILY REFLECTION

Matthew 5:16 NIV
In the same way, let your light shine
before others, that they may see your
good deeds and glorify your
Father in heaven.

WAKE TIME

_____

TODAY'S MANTRA

_____

SCHEDULE

8:00 _____
9:00 _____
10:00 _____
11:00 _____
12:00 _____
13:00 _____
14:00 _____
15:00 _____
16:00 _____
17:00 _____
18:00 _____
19:00 _____
20:00 _____
21:00 _____
22:00 _____
23:00 _____

TOP PRIORITIES

- [ ] _____
- [ ] _____
- [ ] _____

TO-DO LIST

- [ ] _____
- [ ] _____
- [ ] _____
- [ ] _____
- [ ] _____
- [ ] _____
- [ ] _____
- [ ] _____
- [ ] _____
- [ ] _____
- [ ] _____

REFLECTION JOURNAL

DATE _____

First Quarter
Day 1-23 / 3 Weeks

Second Quarter
Day 23-46 / 6-7 Weeks

Third Quarter
Day 46-69 / 7-10 Weeks

Fourth Quarter
Day 69-91 / 10-13 Weeks

Today's Distractions

Today I

_____

_____

_____

_____

_____

_____

_____

_____

PRODUCTIVITY PLANNER

DAILY PRAYER

Help me to love better. Help me to be smarter and make the right decisions . Help me to be more like You. Let Your power shine through me. Amen

DAILY REFLECTION

James 5:16 NIV
Therefore, confess your sins to each other and pray for each other so that you may be healed. The prayer of a righteous person is powerful and effective.

WAKE TIME

_____

TODAY'S MANTRA

_____

SCHEDULE

8:00 _____
9:00 _____
10:00 _____
11:00 _____
12:00 _____
13:00 _____
14:00 _____
15:00 _____
16:00 _____
17:00 _____
18:00 _____
19:00 _____
20:00 _____
21:00 _____
22:00 _____
23:00 _____

TOP PRIORITIES

- ☐ _____
- ☐ _____
- ☐ _____

TO-DO LIST

- ☐ _____
- ☐ _____
- ☐ _____
- ☐ _____
- ☐ _____
- ☐ _____
- ☐ _____
- ☐ _____
- ☐ _____
- ☐ _____
- ☐ _____

REFLECTION JOURNAL

DATE _____

First Quarter
Day 1-23 / 3 Weeks

Second Quarter
Day 23-46 / 6-7 Weeks

Third Quarter
Day 46-69 / 7-10 Weeks

Fourth Quarter
Day 69-91 / 10-13 Weeks

Today's Distractions

Today I

_____

_____

_____

_____

_____

_____

_____

_____

_____

PRODUCTIVITY PLANNER

DAILY PRAYER

I know that this breathe and my existence wouldn't be without you. Remind me that I can do all things through You. Amen

DAILY REFLECTION

Romans 12:8 NIV
if it is to encourage, then give encouragement; if it is giving, then give generously; if it is to lead, do it diligently; if it is to show mercy, do it cheerfully.

WAKE TIME

_____

TODAY'S MANTRA

_____

SCHEDULE

8:00	_____
9:00	_____
10:00	_____
11:00	_____
12:00	_____
13:00	_____
14:00	_____
15:00	_____
16:00	_____
17:00	_____
18:00	_____
19:00	_____
20:00	_____
21:00	_____
22:00	_____
23:00	_____

TOP PRIORITIES

- [ ] _____
- [ ] _____
- [ ] _____

TO-DO LIST

- [ ] _____
- [ ] _____
- [ ] _____
- [ ] _____
- [ ] _____
- [ ] _____
- [ ] _____
- [ ] _____
- [ ] _____
- [ ] _____
- [ ] _____

REFLECTION JOURNAL

DATE _____

First Quarter
Day 1-23 / 3 Weeks

Second Quarter
Day 23-46 / 6-7 Weeks

Third Quarter
Day 46-69 / 7-10 Weeks

Fourth Quarter
Day 69-91 / 10-13 Weeks

Today's Distractions

Today I

_____

_____

_____

_____

_____

_____

_____

_____

PRODUCTIVITY PLANNER

DATE _____

DAILY PRAYER

God guide me. If I get off track, remind me of my purpose. Amen

DAILY REFLECTION

Romans 3:23 NIV
for all have sinned and fall short of the glory of God

WAKE TIME

_____

TODAY'S MANTRA

_____

SCHEDULE

8:00 _____
9:00 _____
10:00 _____
11:00 _____
12:00 _____
13:00 _____
14:00 _____
15:00 _____
16:00 _____
17:00 _____
18:00 _____
19:00 _____
20:00 _____
21:00 _____
22:00 _____
23:00 _____

TOP PRIORITIES

- [ ] _____
- [ ] _____
- [ ] _____

TO-DO LIST

- [ ] _____
- [ ] _____
- [ ] _____
- [ ] _____
- [ ] _____
- [ ] _____
- [ ] _____
- [ ] _____
- [ ] _____
- [ ] _____
- [ ] _____
- [ ] _____

REFLECTION JOURNAL

DATE _____

First Quarter
Day 1-23 / 3 Weeks

Second Quarter
Day 23-46 / 6-7 Weeks

Third Quarter
Day 46-69 / 7-10 Weeks

Fourth Quarter
Day 69-91 / 10-13 Weeks

Today's Distractions

Today I

_____

_____

_____

_____

_____

_____

_____

_____

_____

PRODUCTIVITY PLANNER

DAILY PRAYER

God I thank You for my life, for protecting me, being consistent and loving me unconditionally. Today, I just want to give thanks. Amen

DAILY REFLECTION

Romans 12:19 NIV
Do not take revenge, my dear friends, but leave room for God's wrath, for it is written: "It is mine to avenge; I will repay," says the Lord.

WAKE TIME

_____

TODAY'S MANTRA

_____

SCHEDULE

8:00 _____
9:00 _____
10:00 _____
11:00 _____
12:00 _____
13:00 _____
14:00 _____
15:00 _____
16:00 _____
17:00 _____
18:00 _____
19:00 _____
20:00 _____
21:00 _____
22:00 _____
23:00 _____

TOP PRIORITIES

☐ _____
☐ _____
☐ _____

TO-DO LIST

☐ _____
☐ _____
☐ _____
☐ _____
☐ _____
☐ _____
☐ _____
☐ _____
☐ _____
☐ _____
☐ _____

REFLECTION JOURNAL

DATE _____

First Quarter
Day 1-23 / 3 Weeks

Second Quarter
Day 23-46 / 6-7 Weeks

Third Quarter
Day 46-69 / 7-10 Weeks

Fourth Quarter
Day 69-91 / 10-13 Weeks

Today's Distractions

Today I

_____

_____

_____

_____

_____

_____

_____

_____

PRODUCTIVITY PLANNER

DATE _____

DAILY PRAYER

I want to multiply my productivity and all that I am. Distractions seems to be everywhere. Help me to not bet tempted but to remain focused and to get things done. Amen

DAILY REFLECTION

Matthew 11:28 NIV
"Come to me, all you who are weary and burdened, and I will give you rest.

WAKE TIME

_____

TODAY'S MANTRA

_____

SCHEDULE

8:00 _____
9:00 _____
10:00 _____
11:00 _____
12:00 _____
13:00 _____
14:00 _____
15:00 _____
16:00 _____
17:00 _____
18:00 _____
19:00 _____
20:00 _____
21:00 _____
22:00 _____
23:00 _____

TOP PRIORITIES

- [ ] _____
- [ ] _____
- [ ] _____

TO-DO LIST

- [ ] _____
- [ ] _____
- [ ] _____
- [ ] _____
- [ ] _____
- [ ] _____
- [ ] _____
- [ ] _____
- [ ] _____
- [ ] _____
- [ ] _____
- [ ] _____

REFLECTION JOURNAL

DATE _____

First Quarter
Day 1-23 / 3 Weeks

Second Quarter
Day 23-46 / 6-7 Weeks

Third Quarter
Day 46-69 / 7-10 Weeks

Fourth Quarter
Day 69-91 / 10-13 Weeks

Today's Distractions

Today I

_____

_____

_____

_____

_____

_____

_____

_____

PRODUCTIVITY PLANNER

DAILY PRAYER

Making mistakes can cost me a lot.
I want to be the best version of myself.
Help me to concentrate and not be
distracted or irresponsible. Amen

DAILY REFLECTION

Matthew 11:29 NIV
Take my yoke upon you and learn
from me, for I am gentle and humble
in heart, and you will find rest
for your souls.

WAKE TIME

_____

TODAY'S MANTRA

_____

SCHEDULE

8:00 _____
9:00 _____
10:00 _____
11:00 _____
12:00 _____
13:00 _____
14:00 _____
15:00 _____
16:00 _____
17:00 _____
18:00 _____
19:00 _____
20:00 _____
21:00 _____
22:00 _____
23:00 _____

TOP PRIORITIES

☐ _____
☐ _____
☐ _____

TO-DO LIST

☐ _____
☐ _____
☐ _____
☐ _____
☐ _____
☐ _____
☐ _____
☐ _____
☐ _____
☐ _____
☐ _____

REFLECTION JOURNAL

DATE _____

First Quarter
Day 1-23 / 3 Weeks

Second Quarter
Day 23-46 / 6-7 Weeks

Third Quarter
Day 46-69 / 7-10 Weeks

Fourth Quarter
Day 69-91 / 10-13 Weeks

Today's Distractions

Today I

_____

_____

_____

_____

_____

_____

_____

_____

PRODUCTIVITY PLANNER

DAILY PRAYER

When I want to get things done but feel mentally exhausted, be my strength when I am weak. Give me the energy and mental stamina I need to complete my tasks.
Amen

DAILY REFLECTION

John 14:13 NIV
And I will do whatever you ask
in my name, so that the Father may
be glorified in the Son

WAKE TIME

_____

TODAY'S MANTRA

_____

SCHEDULE

8:00 _____

9:00 _____

10:00 _____

11:00 _____

12:00 _____

13:00 _____

14:00 _____

15:00 _____

16:00 _____

17:00 _____

18:00 _____

19:00 _____

20:00 _____

21:00 _____

22:00 _____

23:00 _____

TOP PRIORITIES

☐ _____

☐ _____

☐ _____

TO-DO LIST

☐ _____

☐ _____

☐ _____

☐ _____

☐ _____

☐ _____

☐ _____

☐ _____

☐ _____

☐ _____

☐ _____

REFLECTION JOURNAL

DATE _____

First Quarter
Day 1-23 / 3 Weeks

Second Quarter
Day 23-46 / 6-7 Weeks

Third Quarter
Day 46-69 / 7-10 Weeks

Fourth Quarter
Day 69-91 / 10-13 Weeks

Today's Distractions

Today I

_____

_____

_____

_____

_____

_____

_____

_____

PRODUCTIVITY PLANNER

DAILY PRAYER

When I worry remind me that I was not created to worry. I'm leaving my fears with You and I trust that You will rebuild me with all the tools I need to do good work and be a provider. Amen

DAILY REFLECTION

1 John 4:18 NIV
There is no fear in love. But perfect love drives out fear, because fear has to do with punishment. The one who fears is not made perfect in love.

WAKE TIME

_____

TODAY'S MANTRA

_____

SCHEDULE

8:00 _____

9:00 _____

10:00 _____

11:00 _____

12:00 _____

13:00 _____

14:00 _____

15:00 _____

16:00 _____

17:00 _____

18:00 _____

19:00 _____

20:00 _____

21:00 _____

22:00 _____

23:00 _____

TOP PRIORITIES

☐ _____

☐ _____

☐ _____

TO-DO LIST

☐ _____

☐ _____

☐ _____

☐ _____

☐ _____

☐ _____

☐ _____

☐ _____

☐ _____

☐ _____

☐ _____

REFLECTION JOURNAL

DATE _____

First Quarter
Day 1-23 / 3 Weeks

Second Quarter
Day 23-46 / 6-7 Weeks

Third Quarter
Day 46-69 / 7-10 Weeks

Fourth Quarter
Day 69-91 / 10-13 Weeks

Today's Distractions

Today I

_____

_____

_____

_____

_____

_____

_____

_____

PRODUCTIVITY PLANNER

DAILY PRAYER

I know that if I had not gone through some rough times, I wouldn't be prepared now for the blessings You are pouring into my life. Help me to stay focused. Amen

DAILY REFLECTION

John 15:5 NIV
"I am the vine; you are the branches. If you remain in me and I in you, you will bear much fruit; apart from me you can do nothing.

WAKE TIME

_____

TODAY'S MANTRA

_____

SCHEDULE

8:00 _____
9:00 _____
10:00 _____
11:00 _____
12:00 _____
13:00 _____
14:00 _____
15:00 _____
16:00 _____
17:00 _____
18:00 _____
19:00 _____
20:00 _____
21:00 _____
22:00 _____
23:00 _____

TOP PRIORITIES

☐ _____
☐ _____
☐ _____

TO-DO LIST

☐ _____
☐ _____
☐ _____
☐ _____
☐ _____
☐ _____
☐ _____
☐ _____
☐ _____
☐ _____
☐ _____

REFLECTION JOURNAL

DATE _____

First Quarter
Day 1-23 / 3 Weeks

Second Quarter
Day 23-46 / 6-7 Weeks

Third Quarter
Day 46-69 / 7-10 Weeks

Fourth Quarter
Day 69-91 / 10-13 Weeks

Today's Distractions

Today I

_____

_____

_____

_____

_____

_____

_____

_____

PRODUCTIVITY PLANNER

DAILY PRAYER

I surrender all my problems to You, all my
concerns. I pray for guidance and peace.
Amen

DAILY REFLECTION

John 15:7 NIV
If you remain in me and my words remain
in you, ask whatever you wish, and it will
be done for you.

WAKE TIME

_____

TODAY'S MANTRA

_____

SCHEDULE

8:00 _____
9:00 _____
10:00 _____
11:00 _____
12:00 _____
13:00 _____
14:00 _____
15:00 _____
16:00 _____
17:00 _____
18:00 _____
19:00 _____
20:00 _____
21:00 _____
22:00 _____
23:00 _____

TOP PRIORITIES

☐ _____
☐ _____
☐ _____

TO-DO LIST

☐ _____
☐ _____
☐ _____
☐ _____
☐ _____
☐ _____
☐ _____
☐ _____
☐ _____
☐ _____
☐ _____
☐ _____

REFLECTION JOURNAL

DATE _____

First Quarter
Day 1-23 / 3 Weeks

Second Quarter
Day 23-46 / 6-7 Weeks

Third Quarter
Day 46-69 / 7-10 Weeks

Fourth Quarter
Day 69-91 / 10-13 Weeks

Today's Distractions

Today I

_____

_____

_____

_____

_____

_____

_____

_____

_____

PRODUCTIVITY PLANNER

DAILY PRAYER

I'm so tired of getting let down. Help me to see that you can turn my pain around. One closed door means a greater door is opening. Turn my discouragement into joy. When people let me down before and I almost gave up, you worked it out all for my good. Keep me focused on You and my purpose. Amen

DAILY REFLECTION

John 16:33 NIV
"I have told you these things, so that in me you may have peace. In this world you will have trouble. But take heart! I have overcome the world."

WAKE TIME

_____

TODAY'S MANTRA

_____

SCHEDULE

8:00	_____
9:00	_____
10:00	_____
11:00	_____
12:00	_____
13:00	_____
14:00	_____
15:00	_____
16:00	_____
17:00	_____
18:00	_____
19:00	_____
20:00	_____
21:00	_____
22:00	_____
23:00	_____

TOP PRIORITIES

- [ ] _____
- [ ] _____
- [ ] _____

TO-DO LIST

- [ ] _____
- [ ] _____
- [ ] _____
- [ ] _____
- [ ] _____
- [ ] _____
- [ ] _____
- [ ] _____
- [ ] _____
- [ ] _____
- [ ] _____
- [ ] _____

REFLECTION JOURNAL

DATE _____

First Quarter
Day 1-23 / 3 Weeks

Second Quarter
Day 23-46 / 6-7 Weeks

Third Quarter
Day 46-69 / 7-10 Weeks

Fourth Quarter
Day 69-91 / 10-13 Weeks

Today's Distractions

Today I

_____

_____

_____

_____

_____

_____

_____

_____

_____

PRODUCTIVITY PLANNER

DAILY PRAYER

So much is going on. I feel distracted, overwhelmed and anxious but I still have fight in me. Give me strength to see things through and not get sidetracked. Amen

DAILY REFLECTION

Jeremiah 29:13 NIV
You will seek me and find me when you seek me with all your heart.

WAKE TIME

_____

TODAY'S MANTRA

_____

SCHEDULE

8:00 _____
9:00 _____
10:00 _____
11:00 _____
12:00 _____
13:00 _____
14:00 _____
15:00 _____
16:00 _____
17:00 _____
18:00 _____
19:00 _____
20:00 _____
21:00 _____
22:00 _____
23:00 _____

TOP PRIORITIES

☐ _____
☐ _____
☐ _____

TO-DO LIST

☐ _____
☐ _____
☐ _____
☐ _____
☐ _____
☐ _____
☐ _____
☐ _____
☐ _____
☐ _____
☐ _____
☐ _____

REFLECTION JOURNAL

DATE _____

First Quarter
Day 1-23 / 3 Weeks

Second Quarter
Day 23-46 / 6-7 Weeks

Third Quarter
Day 46-69 / 7-10 Weeks

Fourth Quarter
Day 69-91 / 10-13 Weeks

Today's Distractions

Today I

_____

_____

_____

_____

_____

_____

_____

_____

PRODUCTIVITY PLANNER

DAILY PRAYER

Everything in my life seems crazy right now but I know You are bigger than any problem. There is nothing too hard for You.
Amen

DAILY REFLECTION

Philippians 4:13 NIV
I can do all this through him who gives me strength.

WAKE TIME

_____

TODAY'S MANTRA

_____

SCHEDULE

8:00 _____

9:00 _____

10:00 _____

11:00 _____

12:00 _____

13:00 _____

14:00 _____

15:00 _____

16:00 _____

17:00 _____

18:00 _____

19:00 _____

20:00 _____

21:00 _____

22:00 _____

23:00 _____

TOP PRIORITIES

☐ _____

☐ _____

☐ _____

TO-DO LIST

☐ _____

☐ _____

☐ _____

☐ _____

☐ _____

☐ _____

☐ _____

☐ _____

☐ _____

☐ _____

☐ _____

REFLECTION JOURNAL

DATE _____

First Quarter
Day 1-23 / 3 Weeks

Second Quarter
Day 23-46 / 6-7 Weeks

Third Quarter
Day 46-69 / 7-10 Weeks

Fourth Quarter
Day 69-91 / 10-13 Weeks

Today's Distractions

Today I

_____

_____

_____

_____

_____

_____

_____

_____

_____

PRODUCTIVITY PLANNER

DAILY PRAYER

God, I love You with my whole heart. Help me to put my hope in You and not man. Thank You for removing all my worrying. I will no longer stress. Amen

DAILY REFLECTION

Philippians 2:13 NIV
for it is God who works in you to will and to act in order to fulfill his good purpose.

WAKE TIME

_____

TODAY'S MANTRA

_____

SCHEDULE

8:00	_____
9:00	_____
10:00	_____
11:00	_____
12:00	_____
13:00	_____
14:00	_____
15:00	_____
16:00	_____
17:00	_____
18:00	_____
19:00	_____
20:00	_____
21:00	_____
22:00	_____
23:00	_____

TOP PRIORITIES

☐ _____
☐ _____
☐ _____

TO-DO LIST

☐ _____
☐ _____
☐ _____
☐ _____
☐ _____
☐ _____
☐ _____
☐ _____
☐ _____
☐ _____
☐ _____
☐ _____

REFLECTION JOURNAL

DATE _____

First Quarter
Day 1-23 / 3 Weeks

Second Quarter
Day 23-46 / 6-7 Weeks

Third Quarter
Day 46-69 / 7-10 Weeks

Fourth Quarter
Day 69-91 / 10-13 Weeks

Today's Distractions

Today I

_____

_____

_____

_____

_____

_____

_____

_____

PRODUCTIVITY PLANNER

DAILY PRAYER

God, I see what you are doing in my life.
Life can be full of surprises but I declare
that everything attach to me wins. Amen

DAILY REFLECTION

Psalms 91:14 NIV
"Because he loves me," says the LORD,
"I will rescue him; I will protect him,
for he acknowledges my name.

WAKE TIME

_____

TODAY'S MANTRA

_____

SCHEDULE

8:00 _____
9:00 _____
10:00 _____
11:00 _____
12:00 _____
13:00 _____
14:00 _____
15:00 _____
16:00 _____
17:00 _____
18:00 _____
19:00 _____
20:00 _____
21:00 _____
22:00 _____
23:00 _____

TOP PRIORITIES

- [ ] _____
- [ ] _____
- [ ] _____

TO-DO LIST

- [ ] _____
- [ ] _____
- [ ] _____
- [ ] _____
- [ ] _____
- [ ] _____
- [ ] _____
- [ ] _____
- [ ] _____
- [ ] _____
- [ ] _____

REFLECTION JOURNAL

DATE _____

First Quarter
Day 1-23 / 3 Weeks

Second Quarter
Day 23-46 / 6-7 Weeks

Third Quarter
Day 46-69 / 7-10 Weeks

Fourth Quarter
Day 69-91 / 10-13 Weeks

Today's Distractions

Today I

_____

_____

_____

_____

_____

_____

_____

_____

_____

PRODUCTIVITY PLANNER

DATE _____

DAILY PRAYER

As I focus on my goals, I pray for hope and for a better future. You are strong and mighty.
As You have planned, help me to walk into my purpose. Amen

DAILY REFLECTION

Psalms 91:15 NIV
He will call on me, and I will answer him;
I will be with him in trouble, I will deliver him and honor him.

WAKE TIME

_____

TODAY'S MANTRA

_____

SCHEDULE

8:00 _____

9:00 _____

10:00 _____

11:00 _____

12:00 _____

13:00 _____

14:00 _____

15:00 _____

16:00 _____

17:00 _____

18:00 _____

19:00 _____

20:00 _____

21:00 _____

22:00 _____

23:00 _____

TOP PRIORITIES

- [ ] _____
- [ ] _____
- [ ] _____

TO-DO LIST

- [ ] _____
- [ ] _____
- [ ] _____
- [ ] _____
- [ ] _____
- [ ] _____
- [ ] _____
- [ ] _____
- [ ] _____
- [ ] _____
- [ ] _____
- [ ] _____

REFLECTION JOURNAL

DATE _____

First Quarter
Day 1-23 / 3 Weeks

Second Quarter
Day 23-46 / 6-7 Weeks

Third Quarter
Day 46-69 / 7-10 Weeks

Fourth Quarter
Day 69-91 / 10-13 Weeks

Today's Distractions

Today I

_____

_____

_____

_____

_____

_____

_____

_____

PRODUCTIVITY PLANNER

DATE _____

DAILY PRAYER

Even when I expect everything to go right, there is
a challenge. Remind me that I am more than a
conquer; I am a survivor. With You I can do all
things. Amen

DAILY REFLECTION

Psalms 51:12 NIV
Restore to me the joy of your salvation
and grant me a willing spirit, to sustain me.

WAKE TIME

_____

TODAY'S MANTRA

_____

SCHEDULE

8:00 _____
9:00 _____
10:00 _____
11:00 _____
12:00 _____
13:00 _____
14:00 _____
15:00 _____
16:00 _____
17:00 _____
18:00 _____
19:00 _____
20:00 _____
21:00 _____
22:00 _____
23:00 _____

TOP PRIORITIES

- [ ] _____
- [ ] _____
- [ ] _____

TO-DO LIST

- [ ] _____
- [ ] _____
- [ ] _____
- [ ] _____
- [ ] _____
- [ ] _____
- [ ] _____
- [ ] _____
- [ ] _____
- [ ] _____
- [ ] _____
- [ ] _____

REFLECTION JOURNAL

DATE _____

First Quarter
Day 1-23 / 3 Weeks

Second Quarter
Day 23-46 / 6-7 Weeks

Third Quarter
Day 46-69 / 7-10 Weeks

Fourth Quarter
Day 69-91 / 10-13 Weeks

Today's Distractions

Today I

_____

_____

_____

_____

_____

_____

_____

_____

PRODUCTIVITY PLANNER

DAILY PRAYER

When a business partner, a love one, job, or my health causes me to feel stressed and unsure. It makes the challenge seem harder and my goals further away. Remind me that I'm not alone or lost without You. Help me to develop healthy and productive relationships with others. Amen

DAILY REFLECTION

Psalms 139:14 NIV
I praise you because I am fearfully and wonderfully made; your works are wonderful; I know that full well.

WAKE TIME

_____

TODAY'S MANTRA

_____

SCHEDULE

8:00 _____
9:00 _____
10:00 _____
11:00 _____
12:00 _____
13:00 _____
14:00 _____
15:00 _____
16:00 _____
17:00 _____
18:00 _____
19:00 _____
20:00 _____
21:00 _____
22:00 _____
23:00 _____

TOP PRIORITIES

☐ _____
☐ _____
☐ _____

TO-DO LIST

☐ _____
☐ _____
☐ _____
☐ _____
☐ _____
☐ _____
☐ _____
☐ _____
☐ _____
☐ _____
☐ _____
☐ _____

REFLECTION JOURNAL

First Quarter
Day 1-23 / 3 Weeks

Second Quarter
Day 23-46 / 6-7 Weeks

Third Quarter
Day 46-69 / 7-10 Weeks

Fourth Quarter
Day 69-91 / 10-13 Weeks

Today's Distractions

Today I

_____

_____

_____

_____

_____

_____

_____

_____

PRODUCTIVITY PLANNER

DAILY PRAYER

The little that I have has been multiplied.
Compared to where I could be, I am truly grateful.
Amen

DAILY REFLECTION

Psalms 37:4 NIV
Take delight in the LORD, and he will give
you the desires of your heart.

WAKE TIME

_____

TODAY'S MANTRA

_____

SCHEDULE

8:00	_____
9:00	_____
10:00	_____
11:00	_____
12:00	_____
13:00	_____
14:00	_____
15:00	_____
16:00	_____
17:00	_____
18:00	_____
19:00	_____
20:00	_____
21:00	_____
22:00	_____
23:00	_____

TOP PRIORITIES

☐ _____
☐ _____
☐ _____

TO-DO LIST

☐ _____
☐ _____
☐ _____
☐ _____
☐ _____
☐ _____
☐ _____
☐ _____
☐ _____
☐ _____
☐ _____

REFLECTION JOURNAL

DATE _____

First Quarter
Day 1-23 / 3 Weeks

Second Quarter
Day 23-46 / 6-7 Weeks

Third Quarter
Day 46-69 / 7-10 Weeks

Fourth Quarter
Day 69-91 / 10-13 Weeks

Today's Distractions

Today I

_____

_____

_____

_____

_____

_____

_____

_____

PRODUCTIVITY PLANNER

DAILY PRAYER

Today I asked that when things are going right, You keep me humble. Purify and clean my heart. So that Your light, can shine through me. Amen

DAILY REFLECTION

Psalms 139:23 NIV
Search me, God, and know my heart; test me and know my anxious thoughts.

WAKE TIME

_____

TODAY'S MANTRA

_____

SCHEDULE

8:00 _____
9:00 _____
10:00 _____
11:00 _____
12:00 _____
13:00 _____
14:00 _____
15:00 _____
16:00 _____
17:00 _____
18:00 _____
19:00 _____
20:00 _____
21:00 _____
22:00 _____
23:00 _____

TOP PRIORITIES

- [ ] _____
- [ ] _____
- [ ] _____

TO-DO LIST

- [ ] _____
- [ ] _____
- [ ] _____
- [ ] _____
- [ ] _____
- [ ] _____
- [ ] _____
- [ ] _____
- [ ] _____
- [ ] _____
- [ ] _____

REFLECTION JOURNAL

DATE _____

First Quarter
Day 1-23 / 3 Weeks

Second Quarter
Day 23-46 / 6-7 Weeks

Third Quarter
Day 46-69 / 7-10 Weeks

Fourth Quarter
Day 69-91 / 10-13 Weeks

Today's Distractions

Today I

_____

_____

_____

_____

_____

_____

_____

_____

PRODUCTIVITY PLANNER

DAILY PRAYER

Today I pray for hope. Hope when things aren't looking good, that they are made better. Hope when the world around me is messed up that it is renewed. Hope when I don't know who to trust that the right people are placed around me. Hope for the desires in my heart to be fulfilled. Amen

DAILY REFLECTION

Psalms 55:22 NIV
Cast your cares on the LORD and he will sustain you; he will never let the righteous be shaken.

WAKE TIME

TODAY'S MANTRA

SCHEDULE

8:00 _____

9:00 _____

10:00 _____

11:00 _____

12:00 _____

13:00 _____

14:00 _____

15:00 _____

16:00 _____

17:00 _____

18:00 _____

19:00 _____

20:00 _____

21:00 _____

22:00 _____

23:00 _____

TOP PRIORITIES

☐ _____

☐ _____

☐ _____

TO-DO LIST

☐ _____

☐ _____

☐ _____

☐ _____

☐ _____

☐ _____

☐ _____

☐ _____

☐ _____

☐ _____

☐ _____

REFLECTION JOURNAL

DATE _____

First Quarter
Day 1-23 / 3 Weeks

Second Quarter
Day 23-46 / 6-7 Weeks

Third Quarter
Day 46-69 / 7-10 Weeks

Fourth Quarter
Day 69-91 / 10-13 Weeks

Today's Distractions

Today I

_____

_____

_____

_____

_____

_____

_____

_____

_____

PRODUCTIVITY PLANNER

DAILY PRAYER

Life can be draining but I can look to You for strength. When I mess up remind me of Your divine power that keeps us moving. I' am only alive today because You allowed it. Remind me of my goals and my purpose and how You are able to blow my mind. Amen

DAILY REFLECTION

Jeremiah 17:5 NIV
This is what the LORD says: "Cursed is the one who trusts in man, who draws strength from mere flesh and whose heart turns away from the LORD.

WAKE TIME

_____

TODAY'S MANTRA

_____

SCHEDULE

8:00 _____
9:00 _____
10:00 _____
11:00 _____
12:00 _____
13:00 _____
14:00 _____
15:00 _____
16:00 _____
17:00 _____
18:00 _____
19:00 _____
20:00 _____
21:00 _____
22:00 _____
23:00 _____

TOP PRIORITIES

☐ _____
☐ _____
☐ _____

TO-DO LIST

☐ _____
☐ _____
☐ _____
☐ _____
☐ _____
☐ _____
☐ _____
☐ _____
☐ _____
☐ _____
☐ _____
☐ _____

REFLECTION JOURNAL

First Quarter
Day 1-23 / 3 Weeks

Second Quarter
Day 23-46 / 6-7 Weeks

Third Quarter
Day 46-69 / 7-10 Weeks

Fourth Quarter
Day 69-91 / 10-13 Weeks

Today's Distractions

Today I

_____

_____

_____

_____

_____

_____

_____

_____

_____

PRODUCTIVITY PLANNER

DAILY PRAYER

Today I just want to give thanks.
Thank You for all the good in my life. Life seems less terrifying with You by my side. Never let me forget how essential You are to my life. Amen

DAILY REFLECTION

Jeremiah 17:10 NIV
"I the LORD search the heart and examine the mind, to reward each person according to their conduct, according to what their deeds deserve."

WAKE TIME

_____

TODAY'S MANTRA

_____

SCHEDULE

8:00 _____
9:00 _____
10:00 _____
11:00 _____
12:00 _____
13:00 _____
14:00 _____
15:00 _____
16:00 _____
17:00 _____
18:00 _____
19:00 _____
20:00 _____
21:00 _____
22:00 _____
23:00 _____

TOP PRIORITIES

☐ _____
☐ _____
☐ _____

TO-DO LIST

☐ _____
☐ _____
☐ _____
☐ _____
☐ _____
☐ _____
☐ _____
☐ _____
☐ _____
☐ _____
☐ _____

REFLECTION JOURNAL

DATE _____

First Quarter
Day 1-23 / 3 Weeks

Second Quarter
Day 23-46 / 6-7 Weeks

Third Quarter
Day 46-69 / 7-10 Weeks

Fourth Quarter
Day 69-91 / 10-13 Weeks

Today's Distractions

Today I

_____

_____

_____

_____

_____

_____

_____

_____

PRODUCTIVITY PLANNER

DAILY PRAYER

Today, God I pray that You rule over all my affairs. When You are involved, even the things I don't understand goes right. Keep me safe, guard my peace and guide my steps. Amen

DAILY REFLECTION

James 1:17 NIV
Every good and perfect gift is from above, coming down from the Father of the heavenly lights, who does not change like shifting shadows.

WAKE TIME

TODAY'S MANTRA

_____

SCHEDULE

8:00	_____
9:00	_____
10:00	_____
11:00	_____
12:00	_____
13:00	_____
14:00	_____
15:00	_____
16:00	_____
17:00	_____
18:00	_____
19:00	_____
20:00	_____
21:00	_____
22:00	_____
23:00	_____

TOP PRIORITIES

☐ _____
☐ _____
☐ _____

TO-DO LIST

☐ _____
☐ _____
☐ _____
☐ _____
☐ _____
☐ _____
☐ _____
☐ _____
☐ _____
☐ _____
☐ _____

REFLECTION JOURNAL

DATE _____

First Quarter
Day 1-23 / 3 Weeks

Second Quarter
Day 23-46 / 6-7 Weeks

Third Quarter
Day 46-69 / 7-10 Weeks

Fourth Quarter
Day 69-91 / 10-13 Weeks

Today's Distractions

Today I

_____

_____

_____

_____

_____

_____

_____

_____

PRODUCTIVITY PLANNER

DAILY PRAYER

In the middle of this challenge, help me to persevere. I've come so far to give up now. God, invade my heart and thoughts with encouragement and faith. I will be victorious and finish the race. Amen

DAILY REFLECTION

Matthew 6:11 NIV
Give us today our daily bread.

WAKE TIME

_____

TODAY'S MANTRA

_____

SCHEDULE

8:00 _____

9:00 _____

10:00 _____

11:00 _____

12:00 _____

13:00 _____

14:00 _____

15:00 _____

16:00 _____

17:00 _____

18:00 _____

19:00 _____

20:00 _____

21:00 _____

22:00 _____

23:00 _____

TOP PRIORITIES

☐ _____

☐ _____

☐ _____

TO-DO LIST

☐ _____

☐ _____

☐ _____

☐ _____

☐ _____

☐ _____

☐ _____

☐ _____

☐ _____

☐ _____

☐ _____

REFLECTION JOURNAL

DATE _____

First Quarter
Day 1-23 / 3 Weeks

Second Quarter
Day 23-46 / 6-7 Weeks

Third Quarter
Day 46-69 / 7-10 Weeks

Fourth Quarter
Day 69-91 / 10-13 Weeks

Today's Distractions

Today I

_____

_____

_____

_____

_____

_____

_____

_____

PRODUCTIVITY PLANNER

DAILY PRAYER

When I can barely fight for myself. God, I pray that You will fight for me, walk with me, lead and counsel me. Help me to go through these hard times gracefully and peacefully. Hear my heart. Remove every burden and renew my strength. Amen

DAILY REFLECTION

Matthew 11:30 NIV
For my yoke is easy and my burden is light.

WAKE TIME

TODAY'S MANTRA

SCHEDULE

8:00 _____

9:00 _____

10:00 _____

11:00 _____

12:00 _____

13:00 _____

14:00 _____

15:00 _____

16:00 _____

17:00 _____

18:00 _____

19:00 _____

20:00 _____

21:00 _____

22:00 _____

23:00 _____

TOP PRIORITIES

☐ _____

☐ _____

☐ _____

TO-DO LIST

☐ _____

☐ _____

☐ _____

☐ _____

☐ _____

☐ _____

☐ _____

☐ _____

☐ _____

☐ _____

☐ _____

REFLECTION JOURNAL

DATE _____

First Quarter
Day 1-23 / 3 Weeks

Second Quarter
Day 23-46 / 6-7 Weeks

Third Quarter
Day 46-69 / 7-10 Weeks

Fourth Quarter
Day 69-91 / 10-13 Weeks

Today's Distractions

Today I

_____

_____

_____

_____

_____

_____

_____

_____

1. **What new skills/strengths have you learned since starting this challenge?**

Do include accomplishments, progress, lessons learned and new developments if any

_____

_____

_____

_____

_____

GRADE CODE

21-22 = 93-100%

19-20 = 90-92%

17-18 = 87-89%

15-16 = 83-86%

13-14 = 80-82%

11-12 = 77-79%

9-10 = 73-76%

7-8 = 70-72%

5-6 = 67-69%

3-4 = 60-66%

0-2 = Below 60%

Assessment: Please check all if any demonstrated during this reporting period

TIME MANAGEMENT

[ ] Engage daily in the Execution routine and activities

[ ] Prioritize time management & organization

[ ] Completed all daily tasks

[ ] Transitions smoothly from preparing to executing task

[ ] Initiated new goals for a future challenge

[ ] Can multitask and meet deadlines

ABILITY

[ ] Implemented plans for personal improvement & growth

[ ] Can prioritize time and avoid distractions

[ ] Uses journal and distractions list

[ ] Uses organizer and planner

[ ] Set clear and specific goals

ATTITUDE

[ ] Can predict outcomes and draw conclusions

[ ] Scheduled time for things I love doing

[ ] Interacted and motivated others to challenge themselves

[ ] Able to refocus when distracted and resume challenge

[ ] Consistently focusing on goals and working towards them daily

PERFORMANCE

[ ] Committed to completing challenge

[ ] Can recognize distractions

[ ] Able to plan naturally

[ ] Completed one goal

[ ] Take notes and plan daily

NAME:

DATE:

PRODUCTIVITY PLANNER

DAILY PRAYER

When things are looking impossible. God remind me that giants do fall. I may not be able to see it happening now but I'm expecting You to make a way. Amen

DAILY REFLECTION

James 1:12 NIV
Blessed is the one who perseveres under trial because, having stood the test, that person will receive the crown of life that the Lord has promised to those who love him.

WAKE TIME

_____

TODAY'S MANTRA

_____

SCHEDULE

8:00	_____
9:00	_____
10:00	_____
11:00	_____
12:00	_____
13:00	_____
14:00	_____
15:00	_____
16:00	_____
17:00	_____
18:00	_____
19:00	_____
20:00	_____
21:00	_____
22:00	_____
23:00	_____

TOP PRIORITIES

- ☐ _____
- ☐ _____
- ☐ _____

TO-DO LIST

- ☐ _____
- ☐ _____
- ☐ _____
- ☐ _____
- ☐ _____
- ☐ _____
- ☐ _____
- ☐ _____
- ☐ _____
- ☐ _____
- ☐ _____
- ☐ _____

REFLECTION JOURNAL

DATE _____

First Quarter
Day 1-23 / 3 Weeks

Second Quarter
Day 23-46 / 6-7 Weeks

Third Quarter
Day 46-69 / 7-10 Weeks

Fourth Quarter
Day 69-91 / 10-13 Weeks

Today's Distractions

Today I

_____

_____

_____

_____

_____

_____

_____

_____

PRODUCTIVITY PLANNER

DATE _____

DAILY PRAYER

When I fear doing things on my own, remind me of Your faithfulness. You would never lead me to leave me alone. I know my faith is being tested. Help me to endure and see it through. Amen

DAILY REFLECTION

Proverbs 12:25 NIV
Anxiety weighs down the heart, but a kind word cheers it up.

WAKE TIME

_____

TODAY'S MANTRA

_____

SCHEDULE

8:00	_____
9:00	_____
10:00	_____
11:00	_____
12:00	_____
13:00	_____
14:00	_____
15:00	_____
16:00	_____
17:00	_____
18:00	_____
19:00	_____
20:00	_____
21:00	_____
22:00	_____
23:00	_____

TOP PRIORITIES

- ☐ _____
- ☐ _____
- ☐ _____

TO-DO LIST

- ☐ _____
- ☐ _____
- ☐ _____
- ☐ _____
- ☐ _____
- ☐ _____
- ☐ _____
- ☐ _____
- ☐ _____
- ☐ _____
- ☐ _____

REFLECTION JOURNAL

DATE _____

First Quarter
Day 1-23 / 3 Weeks

Second Quarter
Day 23-46 / 6-7 Weeks

Third Quarter
Day 46-69 / 7-10 Weeks

Fourth Quarter
Day 69-91 / 10-13 Weeks

Today's Distractions

Today I

_____

_____

_____

_____

_____

_____

_____

_____

PRODUCTIVITY PLANNER

DAILY PRAYER

It seems like distractions are everywhere. Blind my eyes from things that may seem easier but will lead me to destruction. Persevering through my problems refines my character. I look to You for support and strength. Amen

DAILY REFLECTION

Proverbs 4:23 NIV
Above all else, guard your heart, for everything you do flows from it.

WAKE TIME

TODAY'S MANTRA

SCHEDULE

8:00 _____
9:00 _____
10:00 _____
11:00 _____
12:00 _____
13:00 _____
14:00 _____
15:00 _____
16:00 _____
17:00 _____
18:00 _____
19:00 _____
20:00 _____
21:00 _____
22:00 _____
23:00 _____

TOP PRIORITIES

- [ ] _____
- [ ] _____
- [ ] _____

TO-DO LIST

- [ ] _____
- [ ] _____
- [ ] _____
- [ ] _____
- [ ] _____
- [ ] _____
- [ ] _____
- [ ] _____
- [ ] _____
- [ ] _____
- [ ] _____
- [ ] _____

REFLECTION JOURNAL

DATE _____

First Quarter
Day 1-23 / 3 Weeks

Second Quarter
Day 23-46 / 6-7 Weeks

Third Quarter
Day 46-69 / 7-10 Weeks

Fourth Quarter
Day 69-91 / 10-13 Weeks

Today's Distractions

Today I

_____

_____

_____

_____

_____

_____

_____

_____

_____

PRODUCTIVITY PLANNER

DATE _____

DAILY PRAYER

Free me from family curses, hurt, embarrassment and pain. Although I want more for myself, the people around me aren't supportive. Today I pray that You remove any fear that I'm worthless or doubt that I won't overcome. I will be the person You called me to be. Amen

DAILY REFLECTION

Proverbs 16:3 NIV
Commit to the LORD whatever you do, and he will establish your plans.

WAKE TIME

TODAY'S MANTRA

_____

SCHEDULE

8:00	_____
9:00	_____
10:00	_____
11:00	_____
12:00	_____
13:00	_____
14:00	_____
15:00	_____
16:00	_____
17:00	_____
18:00	_____
19:00	_____
20:00	_____
21:00	_____
22:00	_____
23:00	_____

TOP PRIORITIES

☐ _____
☐ _____
☐ _____

TO-DO LIST

☐ _____
☐ _____
☐ _____
☐ _____
☐ _____
☐ _____
☐ _____
☐ _____
☐ _____
☐ _____
☐ _____
☐ _____

REFLECTION JOURNAL

DATE _____

First Quarter
Day 1-23 / 3 Weeks

Second Quarter
Day 23-46 / 6-7 Weeks

Third Quarter
Day 46-69 / 7-10 Weeks

Fourth Quarter
Day 69-91 / 10-13 Weeks

Today's Distractions

Today I

_____

_____

_____

_____

_____

_____

_____

_____

PRODUCTIVITY PLANNER

DATE _____

DAILY PRAYER

There is nothing that's compares to your peace.
I pray that Your presence be with me throughout
the day. Amen

DAILY REFLECTION

Isaiah 9:2 NIV
The people walking in darkness have seen
a great light; on those living in the land
of deep darkness a light has dawned.

WAKE TIME

_____

TODAY'S MANTRA

_____

SCHEDULE

8:00 _____

9:00 _____

10:00 _____

11:00 _____

12:00 _____

13:00 _____

14:00 _____

15:00 _____

16:00 _____

17:00 _____

18:00 _____

19:00 _____

20:00 _____

21:00 _____

22:00 _____

23:00 _____

TOP PRIORITIES

☐ _____

☐ _____

☐ _____

TO-DO LIST

☐ _____

☐ _____

☐ _____

☐ _____

☐ _____

☐ _____

☐ _____

☐ _____

☐ _____

☐ _____

☐ _____

☐ _____

REFLECTION JOURNAL

DATE _____

First Quarter
Day 1-23 / 3 Weeks

Second Quarter
Day 23-46 / 6-7 Weeks

Third Quarter
Day 46-69 / 7-10 Weeks

Fourth Quarter
Day 69-91 / 10-13 Weeks

Today's Distractions

Today I

_____

_____

_____

_____

_____

_____

_____

_____

_____

PRODUCTIVITY PLANNER

DATE _____

DAILY PRAYER

Today I will be encouraged, knowing that everything that I am going through is teaching me to depend on You; You are preparing me for my victory. I will overcome. Amen

DAILY REFLECTION

Isaiah 9:3 NIV
You have enlarged the nation and increased their joy; they rejoice before you as people rejoice at the harvest, as warriors rejoice when dividing the plunder.

WAKE TIME

_____

TODAY'S MANTRA

_____

SCHEDULE

8:00 _____
9:00 _____
10:00 _____
11:00 _____
12:00 _____
13:00 _____
14:00 _____
15:00 _____
16:00 _____
17:00 _____
18:00 _____
19:00 _____
20:00 _____
21:00 _____
22:00 _____
23:00 _____

TOP PRIORITIES

- [ ] _____
- [ ] _____
- [ ] _____

TO-DO LIST

- [ ] _____
- [ ] _____
- [ ] _____
- [ ] _____
- [ ] _____
- [ ] _____
- [ ] _____
- [ ] _____
- [ ] _____
- [ ] _____
- [ ] _____

REFLECTION JOURNAL

DATE _____

First Quarter
Day 1-23 / 3 Weeks

Second Quarter
Day 23-46 / 6-7 Weeks

Third Quarter
Day 46-69 / 7-10 Weeks

Fourth Quarter
Day 69-91 / 10-13 Weeks

Today's Distractions

Today I

_____

_____

_____

_____

_____

_____

_____

_____

PRODUCTIVITY PLANNER

DATE_____

DAILY PRAYER

Today I look to You declaring victory and celebrating in advance because I know You are working everything out for my good.
Amen

DAILY REFLECTION

Isaiah 9:2 NIV
The people walking in darkness have seen a great light; on those living in the land of deep darkness a light has dawned.

WAKE TIME

TODAY'S MANTRA

SCHEDULE

8:00 _____
9:00 _____
10:00 _____
11:00 _____
12:00 _____
13:00 _____
14:00 _____
15:00 _____
16:00 _____
17:00 _____
18:00 _____
19:00 _____
20:00 _____
21:00 _____
22:00 _____
23:00 _____

TOP PRIORITIES

☐ _____
☐ _____
☐ _____

TO-DO LIST

☐ _____
☐ _____
☐ _____
☐ _____
☐ _____
☐ _____
☐ _____
☐ _____
☐ _____
☐ _____
☐ _____
☐ _____

REFLECTION JOURNAL

First Quarter
Day 1-23 / 3 Weeks

Second Quarter
Day 23-46 / 6-7 Weeks

Third Quarter
Day 46-69 / 7-10 Weeks

Fourth Quarter
Day 69-91 / 10-13 Weeks

Today's Distractions

Today I

_____

_____

_____

_____

_____

_____

_____

_____

_____

PRODUCTIVITY PLANNER

DAILY PRAYER

I don't doubt You. I will receive all the great things You've promised. Thank You for the doors You're currently opening in my life and the doors I've never noticed. Amen

DAILY REFLECTION

Isaiah 41:10 NIV
So do not fear, for I am with you; do not be dismayed, for I am your God.
I will strengthen you and help you;
I will uphold you with my righteous right hand.

WAKE TIME

_____

TODAY'S MANTRA

_____

SCHEDULE

8:00 _____
9:00 _____
10:00 _____
11:00 _____
12:00 _____
13:00 _____
14:00 _____
15:00 _____
16:00 _____
17:00 _____
18:00 _____
19:00 _____
20:00 _____
21:00 _____
22:00 _____
23:00 _____

TOP PRIORITIES

☐ _____
☐ _____
☐ _____

TO-DO LIST

☐ _____
☐ _____
☐ _____
☐ _____
☐ _____
☐ _____
☐ _____
☐ _____
☐ _____
☐ _____
☐ _____
☐ _____

REFLECTION JOURNAL

DATE _____

First Quarter
Day 1-23 / 3 Weeks

Second Quarter
Day 23-46 / 6-7 Weeks

Third Quarter
Day 46-69 / 7-10 Weeks

Fourth Quarter
Day 69-91 / 10-13 Weeks

Today's Distractions

Today I

_____

_____

_____

_____

_____

_____

_____

_____

_____

PRODUCTIVITY PLANNER

DAILY PRAYER

When people are trying to weaken my faith and use my current situation to bring me down, remind me of the vision You have for me. The reason I am challenging myself to fulfill Your great purpose. Your will be done. Amen

DAILY REFLECTION

Isaiah 26:3 NIV
You will keep in perfect peace those whose minds are steadfast, because they trust in you.

WAKE TIME

_____

TODAY'S MANTRA

_____

SCHEDULE

8:00 _____

9:00 _____

10:00 _____

11:00 _____

12:00 _____

13:00 _____

14:00 _____

15:00 _____

16:00 _____

17:00 _____

18:00 _____

19:00 _____

20:00 _____

21:00 _____

22:00 _____

23:00 _____

TOP PRIORITIES

☐ _____

☐ _____

☐ _____

TO-DO LIST

☐ _____

☐ _____

☐ _____

☐ _____

☐ _____

☐ _____

☐ _____

☐ _____

☐ _____

☐ _____

☐ _____

☐ _____

REFLECTION JOURNAL

DATE _____

First Quarter
Day 1-23 / 3 Weeks

Second Quarter
Day 23-46 / 6-7 Weeks

Third Quarter
Day 46-69 / 7-10 Weeks

Fourth Quarter
Day 69-91 / 10-13 Weeks

Today's Distractions

Today I

_____

_____

_____

_____

_____

_____

_____

_____

_____

PRODUCTIVITY PLANNER

DAILY PRAYER

When life struggles and my troubles are weighing me down. Help me to keep my mind focused on the unseen turning point of my situation. Amen

DAILY REFLECTION

Isaiah 9:10 NIV
"The bricks have fallen down, but we will rebuild with dressed stone; the fig trees have been felled, but we will replace them with cedars."

WAKE TIME

TODAY'S MANTRA

_____

SCHEDULE

8:00 _____
9:00 _____
10:00 _____
11:00 _____
12:00 _____
13:00 _____
14:00 _____
15:00 _____
16:00 _____
17:00 _____
18:00 _____
19:00 _____
20:00 _____
21:00 _____
22:00 _____
23:00 _____

TOP PRIORITIES

☐ _____
☐ _____
☐ _____

TO-DO LIST

☐ _____
☐ _____
☐ _____
☐ _____
☐ _____
☐ _____
☐ _____
☐ _____
☐ _____
☐ _____
☐ _____

REFLECTION JOURNAL

DATE _____

First Quarter
Day 1-23 / 3 Weeks

Second Quarter
Day 23-46 / 6-7 Weeks

Third Quarter
Day 46-69 / 7-10 Weeks

Fourth Quarter
Day 69-91 / 10-13 Weeks

Today's Distractions

Today I

_____

_____

_____

_____

_____

_____

_____

_____

PRODUCTIVITY PLANNER

DAILY PRAYER

God you are the source of everything good in my life. With You before me, no weapon formed against me will work or cause me any harm. I don't ever want to forget how mighty and great You are. Amen

DAILY REFLECTION

Psalms 145:5 NIV
They speak of the glorious splendor of your majesty— and I will meditate on your wonderful works.

WAKE TIME

_____

TODAY'S MANTRA

_____

SCHEDULE

8:00 _____
9:00 _____
10:00 _____
11:00 _____
12:00 _____
13:00 _____
14:00 _____
15:00 _____
16:00 _____
17:00 _____
18:00 _____
19:00 _____
20:00 _____
21:00 _____
22:00 _____
23:00 _____

TOP PRIORITIES

- [ ] _____
- [ ] _____
- [ ] _____

TO-DO LIST

- [ ] _____
- [ ] _____
- [ ] _____
- [ ] _____
- [ ] _____
- [ ] _____
- [ ] _____
- [ ] _____
- [ ] _____
- [ ] _____
- [ ] _____

REFLECTION JOURNAL

DATE _____

First Quarter
Day 1-23 / 3 Weeks

Second Quarter
Day 23-46 / 6-7 Weeks

Third Quarter
Day 46-69 / 7-10 Weeks

Fourth Quarter
Day 69-91 / 10-13 Weeks

Today's Distractions

Today I

_____

_____

_____

_____

_____

_____

_____

_____

PRODUCTIVITY PLANNER

DAILY PRAYER

I am at peace knowing that although I am uncomfortable now pushing through this challenge; I'm going to be comfortable, proud and ecstatic when I cross the finish line. Help me to make wise and informed decisions. Amen

DAILY REFLECTION

Psalms 105:4 NIV
Look to the LORD and his strength; seek his face always.

WAKE TIME

TODAY'S MANTRA

_____

SCHEDULE

8:00	_____
9:00	_____
10:00	_____
11:00	_____
12:00	_____
13:00	_____
14:00	_____
15:00	_____
16:00	_____
17:00	_____
18:00	_____
19:00	_____
20:00	_____
21:00	_____
22:00	_____
23:00	_____

TOP PRIORITIES

☐ _____
☐ _____
☐ _____

TO-DO LIST

☐ _____
☐ _____
☐ _____
☐ _____
☐ _____
☐ _____
☐ _____
☐ _____
☐ _____
☐ _____
☐ _____

REFLECTION JOURNAL

DATE _____

First Quarter
Day 1-23 / 3 Weeks

Second Quarter
Day 23-46 / 6-7 Weeks

Third Quarter
Day 46-69 / 7-10 Weeks

Fourth Quarter
Day 69-91 / 10-13 Weeks

Today's Distractions

Today I

_____

_____

_____

_____

_____

_____

_____

_____

PRODUCTIVITY PLANNER

DAILY PRAYER

If anything comes in my way to take me off track it is already defeated. It's because of Your power within me that I am able to overcome any challenge. My life has never been my own, humble me and remind me that nothing else matters but You. Amen

DAILY REFLECTION

Isaiah 55:11 NIV
so is my word that goes out from my mouth; It will not return to me empty, but will accomplish what I desire and achieve the purpose for which I sent it.

WAKE TIME

_____

TODAY'S MANTRA

_____

SCHEDULE

8:00	_____
9:00	_____
10:00	_____
11:00	_____
12:00	_____
13:00	_____
14:00	_____
15:00	_____
16:00	_____
17:00	_____
18:00	_____
19:00	_____
20:00	_____
21:00	_____
22:00	_____
23:00	_____

TOP PRIORITIES

- [ ] _____
- [ ] _____
- [ ] _____

TO-DO LIST

- [ ] _____
- [ ] _____
- [ ] _____
- [ ] _____
- [ ] _____
- [ ] _____
- [ ] _____
- [ ] _____
- [ ] _____
- [ ] _____
- [ ] _____
- [ ] _____

REFLECTION JOURNAL

DATE _____

First Quarter
Day 1-23 / 3 Weeks

Second Quarter
Day 23-46 / 6-7 Weeks

Third Quarter
Day 46-69 / 7-10 Weeks

Fourth Quarter
Day 69-91 / 10-13 Weeks

Today's Distractions

Today I

_____

_____

_____

_____

_____

_____

_____

_____

PRODUCTIVITY PLANNER

DAILY PRAYER

I'm grateful not just for the good things, experiences and people, I have but also for the lessons and struggles I had to go through to appreciate where I am today. I am determined to finish the race laid before me. Amen

DAILY REFLECTION

2 Corinthians 9:9 NIV
As it is written: "They have freely scattered their gifts to the poor; their righteousness endures forever."

WAKE TIME

TODAY'S MANTRA

SCHEDULE

8:00 _____
9:00 _____
10:00 _____
11:00 _____
12:00 _____
13:00 _____
14:00 _____
15:00 _____
16:00 _____
17:00 _____
18:00 _____
19:00 _____
20:00 _____
21:00 _____
22:00 _____
23:00 _____

TOP PRIORITIES

- [ ] _____
- [ ] _____
- [ ] _____

TO-DO LIST

- [ ] _____
- [ ] _____
- [ ] _____
- [ ] _____
- [ ] _____
- [ ] _____
- [ ] _____
- [ ] _____
- [ ] _____
- [ ] _____
- [ ] _____
- [ ] _____

REFLECTION JOURNAL

DATE _____

First Quarter
Day 1-23 / 3 Weeks

Second Quarter
Day 23-46 / 6-7 Weeks

Third Quarter
Day 46-69 / 7-10 Weeks

Fourth Quarter
Day 69-91 / 10-13 Weeks

Today's Distractions

Today I

_____

_____

_____

_____

_____

_____

_____

_____

PRODUCTIVITY PLANNER

DATE _____

DAILY PRAYER

Fill my heart and mind with gratitude that flows over into every area of my life. Amen

DAILY REFLECTION

2 Corinthians 9:10 NIV
Now he who supplies seed to the sower and bread for food will also supply and increase your store of seed and will enlarge the harvest of your righteousness.

WAKE TIME

_____

TODAY'S MANTRA

_____

SCHEDULE

8:00 _____

9:00 _____

10:00 _____

11:00 _____

12:00 _____

13:00 _____

14:00 _____

15:00 _____

16:00 _____

17:00 _____

18:00 _____

19:00 _____

20:00 _____

21:00 _____

22:00 _____

23:00 _____

TOP PRIORITIES

☐ _____

☐ _____

☐ _____

TO-DO LIST

☐ _____

☐ _____

☐ _____

☐ _____

☐ _____

☐ _____

☐ _____

☐ _____

☐ _____

☐ _____

☐ _____

REFLECTION JOURNAL

DATE _____

First Quarter
Day 1-23 / 3 Weeks

Second Quarter
Day 23-46 / 6-7 Weeks

Third Quarter
Day 46-69 / 7-10 Weeks

Fourth Quarter
Day 69-91 / 10-13 Weeks

Today's Distractions

Today I

_____

_____

_____

_____

_____

_____

_____

_____

_____

PRODUCTIVITY PLANNER

DAILY PRAYER

Remembering all Your blessings, You have always supplied my needs. You provided food, shelter and protection when I was in need. There is absolutely nobody greater than You. I truly need for nothing. I am grateful for all I have. Amen

DAILY REFLECTION

2 Corinthians 9:11 NIV
You will be enriched in every way so that you can be generous on every occasion, and through us your generosity will result in thanksgiving to God.

WAKE TIME

TODAY'S MANTRA

SCHEDULE

8:00 _____
9:00 _____
10:00 _____
11:00 _____
12:00 _____
13:00 _____
14:00 _____
15:00 _____
16:00 _____
17:00 _____
18:00 _____
19:00 _____
20:00 _____
21:00 _____
22:00 _____
23:00 _____

TOP PRIORITIES

☐ _____
☐ _____
☐ _____

TO-DO LIST

☐ _____
☐ _____
☐ _____
☐ _____
☐ _____
☐ _____
☐ _____
☐ _____
☐ _____
☐ _____
☐ _____
☐ _____

REFLECTION JOURNAL

DATE _____

First Quarter
Day 1-23 / 3 Weeks

Second Quarter
Day 23-46 / 6-7 Weeks

Third Quarter
Day 46-69 / 7-10 Weeks

Fourth Quarter
Day 69-91 / 10-13 Weeks

Today's Distractions

Today I

_____

_____

_____

_____

_____

_____

_____

_____

_____

PRODUCTIVITY PLANNER

DAILY PRAYER

God, today I pray for Your everlasting peace; may it be like a shield around me, protecting and shifting my atmosphere. Amen

DAILY REFLECTION

1 Corinthians 2:9 NIV
However, as it is written: "What no eye has seen, what no ear has heard, and what no human mind has conceived"— the things God has prepared for those who love him

WAKE TIME

_____

TODAY'S MANTRA

_____

SCHEDULE

8:00 _____
9:00 _____
10:00 _____
11:00 _____
12:00 _____
13:00 _____
14:00 _____
15:00 _____
16:00 _____
17:00 _____
18:00 _____
19:00 _____
20:00 _____
21:00 _____
22:00 _____
23:00 _____

TOP PRIORITIES

☐ _____
☐ _____
☐ _____

TO-DO LIST

☐ _____
☐ _____
☐ _____
☐ _____
☐ _____
☐ _____
☐ _____
☐ _____
☐ _____
☐ _____
☐ _____

REFLECTION JOURNAL

DATE _____

First Quarter
Day 1-23 / 3 Weeks

Second Quarter
Day 23-46 / 6-7 Weeks

Third Quarter
Day 46-69 / 7-10 Weeks

Fourth Quarter
Day 69-91 / 10-13 Weeks

Today's Distractions

Today I

_____

_____

_____

_____

_____

_____

_____

_____

_____

PRODUCTIVITY PLANNER

DATE _____

DAILY PRAYER

When I can't see how things are going to
work out, make me aware of Your presence.
I know You got this. I will wait and trust on You.
Amen

DAILY REFLECTION

Ephesians 2:9 NIV
not by works, so that no one can boast.

WAKE TIME

TODAY'S MANTRA

_____

_____

SCHEDULE

8:00	_____
9:00	_____
10:00	_____
11:00	_____
12:00	_____
13:00	_____
14:00	_____
15:00	_____
16:00	_____
17:00	_____
18:00	_____
19:00	_____
20:00	_____
21:00	_____
22:00	_____
23:00	_____

TOP PRIORITIES

☐ _____
☐ _____
☐ _____

TO-DO LIST

☐ _____
☐ _____
☐ _____
☐ _____
☐ _____
☐ _____
☐ _____
☐ _____
☐ _____
☐ _____
☐ _____
☐ _____

REFLECTION JOURNAL

DATE _____

First Quarter
Day 1-23 / 3 Weeks

Second Quarter
Day 23-46 / 6-7 Weeks

Third Quarter
Day 46-69 / 7-10 Weeks

Fourth Quarter
Day 69-91 / 10-13 Weeks

Today's Distractions

Today I

_____

_____

_____

_____

_____

_____

_____

_____

PRODUCTIVITY PLANNER

DAILY PRAYER

As I continue this challenge, continue to fill me until I overflow with Your goodness. Remind me to come to You with all my needs, You are my supplier. Amen

DAILY REFLECTION

Lamentations 3:24 NIV
I say to myself, "The LORD is my portion; therefore, I will wait for him."

WAKE TIME

_____

TODAY'S MANTRA

_____

SCHEDULE

8:00 _____

9:00 _____

10:00 _____

11:00 _____

12:00 _____

13:00 _____

14:00 _____

15:00 _____

16:00 _____

17:00 _____

18:00 _____

19:00 _____

20:00 _____

21:00 _____

22:00 _____

23:00 _____

TOP PRIORITIES

☐ _____

☐ _____

☐ _____

TO-DO LIST

☐ _____

☐ _____

☐ _____

☐ _____

☐ _____

☐ _____

☐ _____

☐ _____

☐ _____

☐ _____

☐ _____

REFLECTION JOURNAL

DATE _____

First Quarter
Day 1-23 / 3 Weeks

Second Quarter
Day 23-46 / 6-7 Weeks

Third Quarter
Day 46-69 / 7-10 Weeks

Fourth Quarter
Day 69-91 / 10-13 Weeks

Today's Distractions

Today I

_____

_____

_____

_____

_____

_____

_____

_____

PRODUCTIVITY PLANNER

DAILY PRAYER

God, You have plans for me that I couldn't even wrap my little brain around. Where You lead me, I will go. I pray that I am not affected by the things of this world. Amen

DAILY REFLECTION

Matthew 6:34 NIV
Therefore, do not worry about tomorrow, for tomorrow will worry about itself. Each day has enough trouble of its own.

WAKE TIME

_____

TODAY'S MANTRA

_____

SCHEDULE

8:00 _____
9:00 _____
10:00 _____
11:00 _____
12:00 _____
13:00 _____
14:00 _____
15:00 _____
16:00 _____
17:00 _____
18:00 _____
19:00 _____
20:00 _____
21:00 _____
22:00 _____
23:00 _____

TOP PRIORITIES

☐ _____
☐ _____
☐ _____

TO-DO LIST

☐ _____
☐ _____
☐ _____
☐ _____
☐ _____
☐ _____
☐ _____
☐ _____
☐ _____
☐ _____
☐ _____

REFLECTION JOURNAL

First Quarter
Day 1-23 / 3 Weeks

Second Quarter
Day 23-46 / 6-7 Weeks

Third Quarter
Day 46-69 / 7-10 Weeks

Fourth Quarter
Day 69-91 / 10-13 Weeks

Today's Distractions

Today I

_____

_____

_____

_____

_____

_____

_____

_____

PRODUCTIVITY PLANNER

DAILY PRAYER

If God is for me then who or what can stand against me. I will fight for my purpose. Amen

DAILY REFLECTION

Psalms 119:105 NIV
Your word is a lamp for my feet, a light on my path.

WAKE TIME

_____

TODAY'S MANTRA

_____

SCHEDULE

8:00 _____

9:00 _____

10:00 _____

11:00 _____

12:00 _____

13:00 _____

14:00 _____

15:00 _____

16:00 _____

17:00 _____

18:00 _____

19:00 _____

20:00 _____

21:00 _____

22:00 _____

23:00 _____

TOP PRIORITIES

☐ _____

☐ _____

☐ _____

TO-DO LIST

☐ _____

☐ _____

☐ _____

☐ _____

☐ _____

☐ _____

☐ _____

☐ _____

☐ _____

☐ _____

☐ _____

REFLECTION JOURNAL

DATE _____

First Quarter
Day 1-23 / 3 Weeks

Second Quarter
Day 23-46 / 6-7 Weeks

Third Quarter
Day 46-69 / 7-10 Weeks

Fourth Quarter
Day 69-91 / 10-13 Weeks

Today's Distractions

Today I

_____

_____

_____

_____

_____

_____

_____

_____

PRODUCTIVITY PLANNER

DATE _____

DAILY PRAYER

During hurtful times I am reminded that
You are always right on time. I will
continue to trust in You. Amen

DAILY REFLECTION

Proverbs 30:5 NIV
"Every word of God is flawless; he is a
shield to those who take refuge in him.

WAKE TIME

TODAY'S MANTRA

_____

SCHEDULE

8:00 _____
9:00 _____
10:00 _____
11:00 _____
12:00 _____
13:00 _____
14:00 _____
15:00 _____
16:00 _____
17:00 _____
18:00 _____
19:00 _____
20:00 _____
21:00 _____
22:00 _____
23:00 _____

TOP PRIORITIES

☐ _____
☐ _____
☐ _____

TO-DO LIST

☐ _____
☐ _____
☐ _____
☐ _____
☐ _____
☐ _____
☐ _____
☐ _____
☐ _____
☐ _____
☐ _____

REFLECTION JOURNAL

DATE _____

First Quarter
Day 1-23 / 3 Weeks

Second Quarter
Day 23-46 / 6-7 Weeks

Third Quarter
Day 46-69 / 7-10 Weeks

Fourth Quarter
Day 69-91 / 10-13 Weeks

Today's Distractions

Today I

_____

_____

_____

_____

_____

_____

_____

_____

_____

PRODUCTIVITY PLANNER

DAILY PRAYER

I'm so amazed at how everything is working out.
I trust that if I would delight myself in You,
You will give me the desires of my heart. Amen

DAILY REFLECTION

John 14:27 NIV
Peace I leave with you; my peace I give you.
I do not give to you as the world gives. Do
not let your hearts be troubled and do not
be afraid.

WAKE TIME

TODAY'S MANTRA

_____

SCHEDULE

8:00	
9:00	
10:00	
11:00	
12:00	
13:00	
14:00	
15:00	
16:00	
17:00	
18:00	
19:00	
20:00	
21:00	
22:00	
23:00	

TOP PRIORITIES

- [ ] _____
- [ ] _____
- [ ] _____

TO-DO LIST

- [ ] _____
- [ ] _____
- [ ] _____
- [ ] _____
- [ ] _____
- [ ] _____
- [ ] _____
- [ ] _____
- [ ] _____
- [ ] _____
- [ ] _____

REFLECTION JOURNAL

DATE _____

First Quarter
Day 1-23 / 3 Weeks

Second Quarter
Day 23-46 / 6-7 Weeks

Third Quarter
Day 46-69 / 7-10 Weeks

Fourth Quarter
Day 69-91 / 10-13 Weeks

Today's Distractions

Today I

_____

_____

_____

_____

_____

_____

_____

_____

PRODUCTIVITY PLANNER

DAILY PRAYER

When I'm feeling stressed and overwhelmed, encourage me to stay strong and focused until I finish this challenge. Amen

DAILY REFLECTION

Psalms 55:23 NIV
But you, God, will bring down the wicked into the pit of decay; the bloodthirsty and deceitful will not live out half their days. But as for me, I trust in you.

WAKE TIME

_____

TODAY'S MANTRA

_____

SCHEDULE

8:00 _____

9:00 _____

10:00 _____

11:00 _____

12:00 _____

13:00 _____

14:00 _____

15:00 _____

16:00 _____

17:00 _____

18:00 _____

19:00 _____

20:00 _____

21:00 _____

22:00 _____

23:00 _____

TOP PRIORITIES

☐ _____

☐ _____

☐ _____

TO-DO LIST

☐ _____

☐ _____

☐ _____

☐ _____

☐ _____

☐ _____

☐ _____

☐ _____

☐ _____

☐ _____

☐ _____

REFLECTION JOURNAL

DATE _____

First Quarter
Day 1-23 / 3 Weeks

Second Quarter
Day 23-46 / 6-7 Weeks

Third Quarter
Day 46-69 / 7-10 Weeks

Fourth Quarter
Day 69-91 / 10-13 Weeks

Today's Distractions

Today I

_____

_____

_____

_____

_____

_____

_____

_____

PRODUCTIVITY PLANNER

DAILY PRAYER

I know the race is just going to get more tough. God guide me and show me the way. When it feels like it's getting a little rocky, help me to stand sure in Your promise for me and endure. Amen

DAILY REFLECTION

Psalms 55:16 NIV
As for me, I call to God, and the LORD saves me.

WAKE TIME

TODAY'S MANTRA

_____

SCHEDULE

8:00 _____
9:00 _____
10:00 _____
11:00 _____
12:00 _____
13:00 _____
14:00 _____
15:00 _____
16:00 _____
17:00 _____
18:00 _____
19:00 _____
20:00 _____
21:00 _____
22:00 _____
23:00 _____

TOP PRIORITIES

- [ ] _____
- [ ] _____
- [ ] _____

TO-DO LIST

- [ ] _____
- [ ] _____
- [ ] _____
- [ ] _____
- [ ] _____
- [ ] _____
- [ ] _____
- [ ] _____
- [ ] _____
- [ ] _____
- [ ] _____
- [ ] _____

REFLECTION JOURNAL

DATE _____

First Quarter
Day 1-23 / 3 Weeks

Second Quarter
Day 23-46 / 6-7 Weeks

Third Quarter
Day 46-69 / 7-10 Weeks

Fourth Quarter
Day 69-91 / 10-13 Weeks

Today's Distractions

Today I

_____

_____

_____

_____

_____

_____

_____

_____

PRODUCTIVITY PLANNER

DAILY PRAYER

Today I want to thank You for the opportunity to be called Your child. I want to live an intentional life that honors You. I want to be so grounded in my purpose; nothing could uproot the blessings You have for my life. Amen

DAILY REFLECTION

Psalms 55:17 NIV
Evening, morning and noon I cry out in distress, and he hears my voice.

WAKE TIME

_____

TODAY'S MANTRA

_____

SCHEDULE

8:00 _____
9:00 _____
10:00 _____
11:00 _____
12:00 _____
13:00 _____
14:00 _____
15:00 _____
16:00 _____
17:00 _____
18:00 _____
19:00 _____
20:00 _____
21:00 _____
22:00 _____
23:00 _____

TOP PRIORITIES

- [ ] _____
- [ ] _____
- [ ] _____

TO-DO LIST

- [ ] _____
- [ ] _____
- [ ] _____
- [ ] _____
- [ ] _____
- [ ] _____
- [ ] _____
- [ ] _____
- [ ] _____
- [ ] _____
- [ ] _____
- [ ] _____

REFLECTION JOURNAL

DATE _____

First Quarter
Day 1-23 / 3 Weeks

Second Quarter
Day 23-46 / 6-7 Weeks

Third Quarter
Day 46-69 / 7-10 Weeks

Fourth Quarter
Day 69-91 / 10-13 Weeks

Today's Distractions

Today I

_____

_____

_____

_____

_____

_____

_____

_____

PRODUCTIVITY PLANNER

DAILY PRAYER

Today I pray that You help me to shine bright and not to hide my gifts. Remind me that I am made in your image and You are alive and active. Amen

DAILY REFLECTION

Psalms 55:18 NIV
He rescues me unharmed from the battle waged against me, even though many oppose me.

WAKE TIME

_____

TODAY'S MANTRA

_____

SCHEDULE

8:00 _____
9:00 _____
10:00 _____
11:00 _____
12:00 _____
13:00 _____
14:00 _____
15:00 _____
16:00 _____
17:00 _____
18:00 _____
19:00 _____
20:00 _____
21:00 _____
22:00 _____
23:00 _____

TOP PRIORITIES

☐ _____
☐ _____
☐ _____

TO-DO LIST

☐ _____
☐ _____
☐ _____
☐ _____
☐ _____
☐ _____
☐ _____
☐ _____
☐ _____
☐ _____
☐ _____

REFLECTION JOURNAL

First Quarter
Day 1-23 / 3 Weeks

Second Quarter
Day 23-46 / 6-7 Weeks

Third Quarter
Day 46-69 / 7-10 Weeks

Fourth Quarter
Day 69-91 / 10-13 Weeks

Today's Distractions

Today I

_____

_____

_____

_____

_____

_____

_____

_____

PRODUCTIVITY PLANNER

DAILY PRAYER

I hear you talking to me and although I can't quite understand it, I see progress. I see the vision. I want to partner with You God in what you're doing in the world around me. Amen

DAILY REFLECTION

Matthew 24:35 NIV
Heaven and earth will pass away, but my words will never pass away.

WAKE TIME

_____

TODAY'S MANTRA

_____

SCHEDULE

8:00	_____
9:00	_____
10:00	_____
11:00	_____
12:00	_____
13:00	_____
14:00	_____
15:00	_____
16:00	_____
17:00	_____
18:00	_____
19:00	_____
20:00	_____
21:00	_____
22:00	_____
23:00	_____

TOP PRIORITIES

☐ _____
☐ _____
☐ _____

TO-DO LIST

☐ _____
☐ _____
☐ _____
☐ _____
☐ _____
☐ _____
☐ _____
☐ _____
☐ _____
☐ _____
☐ _____

REFLECTION JOURNAL

DATE _____

First Quarter
Day 1-23 / 3 Weeks

Second Quarter
Day 23-46 / 6-7 Weeks

Third Quarter
Day 46-69 / 7-10 Weeks

Fourth Quarter
Day 69-91 / 10-13 Weeks

Today's Distractions

Today I

_____

_____

_____

_____

_____

_____

_____

_____

PRODUCTIVITY PLANNER

DAILY PRAYER

I just want to give thanks. Everything isn't going as I planned but God, You are so good. Your words have the power to transform my life and this world. Amen

DAILY REFLECTION

Joshua 1:9 NIV
Have I not commanded you? Be strong and courageous. Do not be afraid; do not be discouraged, for the LORD your God will be with you wherever you go."

WAKE TIME

_____

TODAY'S MANTRA

_____

SCHEDULE

8:00 _____
9:00 _____
10:00 _____
11:00 _____
12:00 _____
13:00 _____
14:00 _____
15:00 _____
16:00 _____
17:00 _____
18:00 _____
19:00 _____
20:00 _____
21:00 _____
22:00 _____
23:00 _____

TOP PRIORITIES

☐ _____
☐ _____
☐ _____

TO-DO LIST

☐ _____
☐ _____
☐ _____
☐ _____
☐ _____
☐ _____
☐ _____
☐ _____
☐ _____
☐ _____
☐ _____
☐ _____

REFLECTION JOURNAL

DATE _____

First Quarter
Day 1-23 / 3 Weeks

Second Quarter
Day 23-46 / 6-7 Weeks

Third Quarter
Day 46-69 / 7-10 Weeks

Fourth Quarter
Day 69-91 / 10-13 Weeks

Today's Distractions

Today I

_____

_____

_____

_____

_____

_____

_____

_____

PRODUCTIVITY PLANNER

DAILY PRAYER

When I am discouraged, God help me to always believe in your word. Help me to remember that I am in good hands. Amen

DAILY REFLECTION

Romans 5:3-4 NIV
Not only so, but we also glory in our sufferings, because we know that suffering produces perseverance. perseverance, character; and character, hope.

WAKE TIME

_____

TODAY'S MANTRA

_____

SCHEDULE

8:00 _____

9:00 _____

10:00 _____

11:00 _____

12:00 _____

13:00 _____

14:00 _____

15:00 _____

16:00 _____

17:00 _____

18:00 _____

19:00 _____

20:00 _____

21:00 _____

22:00 _____

23:00 _____

TOP PRIORITIES

☐ _____

☐ _____

☐ _____

TO-DO LIST

☐ _____

☐ _____

☐ _____

☐ _____

☐ _____

☐ _____

☐ _____

☐ _____

☐ _____

☐ _____

☐ _____

REFLECTION JOURNAL

DATE _____

First Quarter
Day 1-23 / 3 Weeks

Second Quarter
Day 23-46 / 6-7 Weeks

Third Quarter
Day 46-69 / 7-10 Weeks

Fourth Quarter
Day 69-91 / 10-13 Weeks

Today's Distractions

Today I

_____

_____

_____

_____

_____

_____

_____

_____

_____

PRODUCTIVITY PLANNER

DAILY PRAYER

When distractions come my way. Remind me of my purpose and help me to refocus. Align my life with Your word. Amen

DAILY REFLECTION

Romans 8:24 NIV
For in this hope, we were saved. But hope that is seen is no hope at all. Who hopes for what they already have?

WAKE TIME

_____

TODAY'S MANTRA

_____

SCHEDULE

8:00 _____
9:00 _____
10:00 _____
11:00 _____
12:00 _____
13:00 _____
14:00 _____
15:00 _____
16:00 _____
17:00 _____
18:00 _____
19:00 _____
20:00 _____
21:00 _____
22:00 _____
23:00 _____

TOP PRIORITIES

- [ ] _____
- [ ] _____
- [ ] _____

TO-DO LIST

- [ ] _____
- [ ] _____
- [ ] _____
- [ ] _____
- [ ] _____
- [ ] _____
- [ ] _____
- [ ] _____
- [ ] _____
- [ ] _____
- [ ] _____
- [ ] _____

REFLECTION JOURNAL

DATE _____

First Quarter
Day 1-23 / 3 Weeks

Second Quarter
Day 23-46 / 6-7 Weeks

Third Quarter
Day 46-69 / 7-10 Weeks

Fourth Quarter
Day 69-91 / 10-13 Weeks

Today's Distractions

Today I

_____

_____

_____

_____

_____

_____

_____

_____

PRODUCTIVITY PLANNER

DAILY PRAYER

Every day I trust in God. You have shown Yourself faithful, kind, trustworthy and a true friend in my time of need. Thank You for being a friend. Amen

DAILY REFLECTION

Romans 15:13 NIV
May the God of hope fill you with all joy and peace as you trust in him, so that you may overflow with hope by the power of the Holy Spirit.

WAKE TIME

_____

TODAY'S MANTRA

_____

SCHEDULE

8:00	_____
9:00	_____
10:00	_____
11:00	_____
12:00	_____
13:00	_____
14:00	_____
15:00	_____
16:00	_____
17:00	_____
18:00	_____
19:00	_____
20:00	_____
21:00	_____
22:00	_____
23:00	_____

TOP PRIORITIES

- ☐ _____
- ☐ _____
- ☐ _____

TO-DO LIST

- ☐ _____
- ☐ _____
- ☐ _____
- ☐ _____
- ☐ _____
- ☐ _____
- ☐ _____
- ☐ _____
- ☐ _____
- ☐ _____
- ☐ _____

REFLECTION JOURNAL

DATE _____

First Quarter
Day 1-23 / 3 Weeks

Second Quarter
Day 23-46 / 6-7 Weeks

Third Quarter
Day 46-69 / 7-10 Weeks

Fourth Quarter
Day 69-91 / 10-13 Weeks

Today's Distractions

Today I

_____

_____

_____

_____

_____

_____

_____

_____

PRODUCTIVITY PLANNER

DAILY PRAYER

The payoff is coming, help me not to give up now. I believe that my time is right now.
All that I'm doing will be a blessing to my family, friends, businesses, communities, physical, emotional, financial and mental health. Amen

DAILY REFLECTION

Matthew 6:27 NIV
Can any one of you by worrying add a single hour to your life?

WAKE TIME

_____

TODAY'S MANTRA

_____

SCHEDULE

8:00 _____

9:00 _____

10:00 _____

11:00 _____

12:00 _____

13:00 _____

14:00 _____

15:00 _____

16:00 _____

17:00 _____

18:00 _____

19:00 _____

20:00 _____

21:00 _____

22:00 _____

23:00 _____

TOP PRIORITIES

☐ _____

☐ _____

☐ _____

TO-DO LIST

☐ _____

☐ _____

☐ _____

☐ _____

☐ _____

☐ _____

☐ _____

☐ _____

☐ _____

☐ _____

☐ _____

☐ _____

REFLECTION JOURNAL

DATE _____

First Quarter
Day 1-23 / 3 Weeks

Second Quarter
Day 23-46 / 6-7 Weeks

Third Quarter
Day 46-69 / 7-10 Weeks

Fourth Quarter
Day 69-91 / 10-13 Weeks

Today's Distractions

Today I

_____

_____

_____

_____

_____

_____

_____

_____

PRODUCTIVITY PLANNER

DAILY PRAYER

If and when I feel doubtful, anxious, impatient, unmotivated, or overwhelmed, God remind me that You are above all things and You hold all things together. Lead me to my purpose. Amen

DAILY REFLECTION

Psalms 119:104 NIV
I gain understanding from your precepts; therefore, I hate every wrong path.

WAKE TIME

_____

TODAY'S MANTRA

_____

SCHEDULE

8:00 _____
9:00 _____
10:00 _____
11:00 _____
12:00 _____
13:00 _____
14:00 _____
15:00 _____
16:00 _____
17:00 _____
18:00 _____
19:00 _____
20:00 _____
21:00 _____
22:00 _____
23:00 _____

TOP PRIORITIES

- ☐ _____
- ☐ _____
- ☐ _____

TO-DO LIST

- ☐ _____
- ☐ _____
- ☐ _____
- ☐ _____
- ☐ _____
- ☐ _____
- ☐ _____
- ☐ _____
- ☐ _____
- ☐ _____
- ☐ _____

REFLECTION JOURNAL

DATE _____

First Quarter
Day 1-23 / 3 Weeks

Second Quarter
Day 23-46 / 6-7 Weeks

Third Quarter
Day 46-69 / 7-10 Weeks

Fourth Quarter
Day 69-91 / 10-13 Weeks

Today's Distractions

Today I

_____

_____

_____

_____

_____

_____

_____

_____

PRODUCTIVITY PLANNER

DAILY PRAYER

Today I pray specifically over my life and health. Show me how I can be of service with my life. Give me wisdom when making decisions and selecting healthy relationships. When I slip up and get off track remind me that You are my rock and peace. Amen

DAILY REFLECTION

Psalms 18:28 NIV
You, LORD, keep my lamp burning; my God turns my darkness into light.

WAKE TIME

_____

TODAY'S MANTRA

_____

SCHEDULE

8:00 _____
9:00 _____
10:00 _____
11:00 _____
12:00 _____
13:00 _____
14:00 _____
15:00 _____
16:00 _____
17:00 _____
18:00 _____
19:00 _____
20:00 _____
21:00 _____
22:00 _____
23:00 _____

TOP PRIORITIES

☐ _____
☐ _____
☐ _____

TO-DO LIST

☐ _____
☐ _____
☐ _____
☐ _____
☐ _____
☐ _____
☐ _____
☐ _____
☐ _____
☐ _____
☐ _____
☐ _____

REFLECTION JOURNAL

DATE _____

First Quarter
Day 1-23 / 3 Weeks

Second Quarter
Day 23-46 / 6-7 Weeks

Third Quarter
Day 46-69 / 7-10 Weeks

Fourth Quarter
Day 69-91 / 10-13 Weeks

Today's Distractions

Today I

_____

_____

_____

_____

_____

_____

_____

_____

PRODUCTIVITY PLANNER

DAILY PRAYER

I put my trust in You. Today I pray that You put Your trust in me and send me. Amen

DAILY REFLECTION

Matthew 5:14 NIV
"You are the light of the world. A town built on a hill cannot be hidden.

WAKE TIME

_____

TODAY'S MANTRA

_____

SCHEDULE

8:00 _____

9:00 _____

10:00 _____

11:00 _____

12:00 _____

13:00 _____

14:00 _____

15:00 _____

16:00 _____

17:00 _____

18:00 _____

19:00 _____

20:00 _____

21:00 _____

22:00 _____

23:00 _____

TOP PRIORITIES

☐ _____

☐ _____

☐ _____

TO-DO LIST

☐ _____

☐ _____

☐ _____

☐ _____

☐ _____

☐ _____

☐ _____

☐ _____

☐ _____

☐ _____

☐ _____

REFLECTION JOURNAL

DATE _____

First Quarter
Day 1-23 / 3 Weeks

Second Quarter
Day 23-46 / 6-7 Weeks

Third Quarter
Day 46-69 / 7-10 Weeks

Fourth Quarter
Day 69-91 / 10-13 Weeks

Today's Distractions

Today I

_____

_____

_____

_____

_____

_____

_____

_____

_____

PRODUCTIVITY PLANNER

DATE _____

DAILY PRAYER

Today I ask that you show me the paths that lead to restoration and fulfillment. Guide my feet and hands. Open or shield my eyes and ears. I will handle these hardships and come out strong. Amen

DAILY REFLECTION

Matthew 5:15 NIV
Neither do people light a lamp and put it under a bowl. Instead, they put it on its stand, and it gives light to everyone in the house.

WAKE TIME

TODAY'S MANTRA

_____

SCHEDULE

8:00 _____
9:00 _____
10:00 _____
11:00 _____
12:00 _____
13:00 _____
14:00 _____
15:00 _____
16:00 _____
17:00 _____
18:00 _____
19:00 _____
20:00 _____
21:00 _____
22:00 _____
23:00 _____

TOP PRIORITIES

- [ ] _____
- [ ] _____
- [ ] _____

TO-DO LIST

- [ ] _____
- [ ] _____
- [ ] _____
- [ ] _____
- [ ] _____
- [ ] _____
- [ ] _____
- [ ] _____
- [ ] _____
- [ ] _____
- [ ] _____
- [ ] _____

REFLECTION JOURNAL

DATE _____

First Quarter
Day 1-23 / 3 Weeks

Second Quarter
Day 23-46 / 6-7 Weeks

Third Quarter
Day 46-69 / 7-10 Weeks

Fourth Quarter
Day 69-91 / 10-13 Weeks

Today's Distractions

Today I

_____

_____

_____

_____

_____

_____

_____

_____

PRODUCTIVITY PLANNER

DAILY PRAYER

Yesterday, today and forever, You are God.
Therefore, I will honor You all the days of my life.
All praises belong to you. Amen

DAILY REFLECTION

1 Peter 2:9 NIV
But you are a chosen people, a royal
priesthood, a holy nation, God's special
possession, that you may declare the
praises of him who called you out of
darkness into his wonderful light.

WAKE TIME

TODAY'S MANTRA

_____

SCHEDULE

8:00 _____
9:00 _____
10:00 _____
11:00 _____
12:00 _____
13:00 _____
14:00 _____
15:00 _____
16:00 _____
17:00 _____
18:00 _____
19:00 _____
20:00 _____
21:00 _____
22:00 _____
23:00 _____

TOP PRIORITIES

☐ _____
☐ _____
☐ _____

TO-DO LIST

☐ _____
☐ _____
☐ _____
☐ _____
☐ _____
☐ _____
☐ _____
☐ _____
☐ _____
☐ _____
☐ _____
☐ _____

REFLECTION JOURNAL

DATE _____

First Quarter
Day 1-23 / 3 Weeks

Second Quarter
Day 23-46 / 6-7 Weeks

Third Quarter
Day 46-69 / 7-10 Weeks

Fourth Quarter
Day 69-91 / 10-13 Weeks

Today's Distractions

Today I

_____

_____

_____

_____

_____

_____

_____

_____

_____

PRODUCTIVITY PLANNER

DATE _____

DAILY PRAYER

May my life be filled from the inside so that the blessings overflow into lives of others. Amen

DAILY REFLECTION

Luke 12:40 NIV
You also must be ready, because the Son of Man will come at an hour when you do not expect him."

WAKE TIME

_____

TODAY'S MANTRA

_____

SCHEDULE

8:00 _____
9:00 _____
10:00 _____
11:00 _____
12:00 _____
13:00 _____
14:00 _____
15:00 _____
16:00 _____
17:00 _____
18:00 _____
19:00 _____
20:00 _____
21:00 _____
22:00 _____
23:00 _____

TOP PRIORITIES

- [ ] _____
- [ ] _____
- [ ] _____

TO-DO LIST

- [ ] _____
- [ ] _____
- [ ] _____
- [ ] _____
- [ ] _____
- [ ] _____
- [ ] _____
- [ ] _____
- [ ] _____
- [ ] _____
- [ ] _____

REFLECTION JOURNAL

DATE _____

First Quarter
Day 1-23 / 3 Weeks

Second Quarter
Day 23-46 / 6-7 Weeks

Third Quarter
Day 46-69 / 7-10 Weeks

Fourth Quarter
Day 69-91 / 10-13 Weeks

Today's Distractions

Today I

_____

_____

_____

_____

_____

_____

_____

_____

_____

PRODUCTIVITY PLANNER

DATE _____

DAILY PRAYER

Give me the boldness to honor You with my time, money and life. I pray that I am so dedicated to my purpose that only You can distract me. Amen

DAILY REFLECTION

Hebrews 12:28 NIV
Therefore, since we are receiving a kingdom that cannot be shaken, let us be thankful,and so worship God acceptably with reverence and awe for our "God is a consuming fire."

WAKE TIME

_____

TODAY'S MANTRA

_____

SCHEDULE

8:00 _____

9:00 _____

10:00 _____

11:00 _____

12:00 _____

13:00 _____

14:00 _____

15:00 _____

16:00 _____

17:00 _____

18:00 _____

19:00 _____

20:00 _____

21:00 _____

22:00 _____

23:00 _____

TOP PRIORITIES

☐ _____

☐ _____

☐ _____

TO-DO LIST

☐ _____

☐ _____

☐ _____

☐ _____

☐ _____

☐ _____

☐ _____

☐ _____

☐ _____

☐ _____

☐ _____

REFLECTION JOURNAL

DATE _____

First Quarter
Day 1-23 / 3 Weeks

Second Quarter
Day 23-46 / 6-7 Weeks

Third Quarter
Day 46-69 / 7-10 Weeks

Fourth Quarter
Day 69-91 / 10-13 Weeks

Today's Distractions

Today I

_____

_____

_____

_____

_____

_____

_____

_____

PRODUCTIVITY PLANNER

DAILY PRAYER

Today, show me what to invest my money and time in and help me to give generously and humbly. Amen

DAILY REFLECTION

Jeremiah 17:10 NIV
"I the LORD search the heart and examine the mind, to reward each person according to their conduct, according to what their deeds deserve."

WAKE TIME

_____

TODAY'S MANTRA

_____

SCHEDULE

8:00 _____
9:00 _____
10:00 _____
11:00 _____
12:00 _____
13:00 _____
14:00 _____
15:00 _____
16:00 _____
17:00 _____
18:00 _____
19:00 _____
20:00 _____
21:00 _____
22:00 _____
23:00 _____

TOP PRIORITIES

- [ ] _____
- [ ] _____
- [ ] _____

TO-DO LIST

- [ ] _____
- [ ] _____
- [ ] _____
- [ ] _____
- [ ] _____
- [ ] _____
- [ ] _____
- [ ] _____
- [ ] _____
- [ ] _____
- [ ] _____
- [ ] _____

REFLECTION JOURNAL

DATE _____

First Quarter
Day 1-23 / 3 Weeks

Second Quarter
Day 23-46 / 6-7 Weeks

Third Quarter
Day 46-69 / 7-10 Weeks

Fourth Quarter
Day 69-91 / 10-13 Weeks

Today's Distractions

Today I

_____

_____

_____

_____

_____

_____

_____

_____

PRODUCTIVITY PLANNER

DAILY PRAYER

Today I pray for myself and the world.
Every attack that causes harm, frustration and
destruction; I pray it be blocked.
Amen

DAILY REFLECTION

Philippians 4:6 NIV
Do not be anxious about anything, but in
every situation, by prayer and petition,
with thanksgiving, present your requests to
God.

WAKE TIME

TODAY'S MANTRA

SCHEDULE

8:00 _____

9:00 _____

10:00 _____

11:00 _____

12:00 _____

13:00 _____

14:00 _____

15:00 _____

16:00 _____

17:00 _____

18:00 _____

19:00 _____

20:00 _____

21:00 _____

22:00 _____

23:00 _____

TOP PRIORITIES

☐ _____

☐ _____

☐ _____

TO-DO LIST

☐ _____

☐ _____

☐ _____

☐ _____

☐ _____

☐ _____

☐ _____

☐ _____

☐ _____

☐ _____

☐ _____

REFLECTION JOURNAL

DATE _____

First Quarter
Day 1-23 / 3 Weeks

Second Quarter
Day 23-46 / 6-7 Weeks

Third Quarter
Day 46-69 / 7-10 Weeks

Fourth Quarter
Day 69-91 / 10-13 Weeks

Today's Distractions

Today I

_____

_____

_____

_____

_____

_____

_____

_____

PRODUCTIVITY PLANNER

DATE _____

DAILY PRAYER

As I come closer to finishing this challenge,
I ask that You keep me vigilant and help me
to avoid traps and roads that lead to destruction.
Remind me that You are in control. Amen

DAILY REFLECTION

Philippians 4:13 NIV
I can do all this through him who gives me
strength.

WAKE TIME

_____

TODAY'S MANTRA

_____

SCHEDULE

8:00 _____

9:00 _____

10:00 _____

11:00 _____

12:00 _____

13:00 _____

14:00 _____

15:00 _____

16:00 _____

17:00 _____

18:00 _____

19:00 _____

20:00 _____

21:00 _____

22:00 _____

23:00 _____

TOP PRIORITIES

☐ _____

☐ _____

☐ _____

TO-DO LIST

☐ _____

☐ _____

☐ _____

☐ _____

☐ _____

☐ _____

☐ _____

☐ _____

☐ _____

☐ _____

☐ _____

REFLECTION JOURNAL

DATE _____

First Quarter
Day 1-23 / 3 Weeks

Second Quarter
Day 23-46 / 6-7 Weeks

Third Quarter
Day 46-69 / 7-10 Weeks

Fourth Quarter
Day 69-91 / 10-13 Weeks

Today's Distractions

Today I

_____

_____

_____

_____

_____

_____

_____

_____

_____

PRODUCTIVITY PLANNER

DATE _____

DAILY PRAYER

No matter what I go through, after this challenge. Remind me that I am not alone. I am seen and loved by You. I am humbled by this journey and Your sacrificial commitment to our relationship. Other people may have let me down or given up on me but You saw me through. Whenever I would wander away, You always found me and put me right back on track. Continue to walk with me. Amen

DAILY REFLECTION

Psalms 150:6 NIV
Let everything that has breath praise the LORD. Praise the LORD.

WAKE TIME

_____

SCHEDULE

8:00 _____

9:00 _____

10:00 _____

11:00 _____

12:00 _____

13:00 _____

14:00 _____

15:00 _____

16:00 _____

17:00 _____

18:00 _____

19:00 _____

20:00 _____

21:00 _____

22:00 _____

23:00 _____

TODAY'S MANTRA

_____

TOP PRIORITIES

☐ _____

☐ _____

☐ _____

TO-DO LIST

☐ _____

☐ _____

☐ _____

☐ _____

☐ _____

☐ _____

☐ _____

☐ _____

☐ _____

☐ _____

☐ _____

REFLECTION JOURNAL

DATE _____

First Quarter
Day 1-23 / 3 Weeks

Second Quarter
Day 23-46 / 6-7 Weeks

Third Quarter
Day 46-69 / 7-10 Weeks

Fourth Quarter
Day 69-91 / 10-13 Weeks

Today's Distractions

Today I

_____

_____

_____

_____

_____

_____

_____

_____

PRODUCTIVITY PLANNER

DAILY PRAYER

I am grateful for this challenge. It was not easy but again I proven that I can do all things through God that strengthens me. I'm excited for this new chapter in my life. God, You have empowered and equipped me with everything I need to fulfill Your purpose throughout my lifetime. Amen

DAILY REFLECTION

Romans 15:13 NIV
May the God of hope fill you with all joy and peace as you trust in him, so that you may overflow with hope by the power of the Holy Spirit.

WAKE TIME

_____

TODAY'S MANTRA

_____

SCHEDULE

8:00	_____
9:00	_____
10:00	_____
11:00	_____
12:00	_____
13:00	_____
14:00	_____
15:00	_____
16:00	_____
17:00	_____
18:00	_____
19:00	_____
20:00	_____
21:00	_____
22:00	_____
23:00	_____

TOP PRIORITIES

☐ _____
☐ _____
☐ _____

TO-DO LIST

☐ _____
☐ _____
☐ _____
☐ _____
☐ _____
☐ _____
☐ _____
☐ _____
☐ _____
☐ _____
☐ _____
☐ _____

REFLECTION JOURNAL

DATE _____

First Quarter
Day 1-23 / 3 Weeks

Second Quarter
Day 23-46 / 6-7 Weeks

Third Quarter
Day 46-69 / 7-10 Weeks

Fourth Quarter
Day 69-91 / 10-13 Weeks

Today's Distractions

Today I

_____

_____

_____

_____

_____

_____

_____

_____

PRODUCTIVITY PLANNER

DAILY PRAYER

When I am feeling depressed, discouraged, stressed, overwhelmed teach me how to deal with people in healthy ways. Comfort me as I go forward in life. Give me the boldness to remain true to You. Align my heart and mind with your will. May grace, mercy and peace be with me all the days of my life. Amen

DAILY REFLECTION

Romans 8:26 NIV
In the same way, the Spirit helps us in our weakness. We do not know what we ought to pray for, but the Spirit himself intercedes for us through wordless groans.

WAKE TIME

_____

TODAY'S MANTRA

_____

SCHEDULE

8:00 _____

9:00 _____

10:00 _____

11:00 _____

12:00 _____

13:00 _____

14:00 _____

15:00 _____

16:00 _____

17:00 _____

18:00 _____

19:00 _____

20:00 _____

21:00 _____

22:00 _____

23:00 _____

TOP PRIORITIES

☐ _____

☐ _____

☐ _____

TO-DO LIST

☐ _____

☐ _____

☐ _____

☐ _____

☐ _____

☐ _____

☐ _____

☐ _____

☐ _____

☐ _____

☐ _____

REFLECTION JOURNAL

First Quarter
Day 1-23 / 3 Weeks

Second Quarter
Day 23-46 / 6-7 Weeks

Third Quarter
Day 46-69 / 7-10 Weeks

Fourth Quarter
Day 69-91 / 10-13 Weeks

Today's Distractions

Today I

_____

_____

_____

_____

_____

_____

_____

_____

1. *How are my 5 goals being filled?*

Do include accomplishments, progress, lessons learned and new developments if any

_____

_____

_____

_____

_____

GRADE CODE

21–22 =	93–100%
19–20 =	90–92%
17–18 =	87–89%
15–16 =	83–86%
13–14 =	80–82%
11–12 =	77–79%
9–10 =	73–76%
7–8 =	70–72%
5–6 =	67–69%
3–4 =	60–66%
0–2 =	Below 60%

Assessment: Please check all if any demonstrated during this reporting period

TIME MANAGEMENT

[ ] Engage daily in the Execution routine and activities

[ ] Prioritize time management & organization

[ ] Completed all daily tasks

[ ] Transitions smoothly from preparing to executing task

[ ] Initiated new goals for a future challenge

[ ] Multitasking and meeting deadlines

ABILITY

[ ] Implemented plans for personal improvement & growth

[ ] Prioritize time and avoid distractions

[ ] Uses journal and distractions list

[ ] Uses organizer and planner

[ ] Set clear and specific goals

ATTITUDE

[ ] Predicts outcomes and draw conclusions

[ ] Scheduled time for things I love doing

[ ] Interacted and motivated others to challenge themselves

[ ] Able to refocus when distracted and resume challenge

[ ] Consistently focusing on goals and working towards them daily

PERFORMANCE

[ ] Completed challenge

[ ] Can naturally recognize distractions

[ ] Able to plan naturally

[ ] Completed all 5 goals

[ ] Take notes and plan daily

NAME:

DATE:

I'm All Ears!

GOOD NEWS IS INFECTIOUS!
Your story can touch others in ways
you could not begin to imagine.
I'd love to hear your story on how
you overcame this challenge.

Send comments, testimonies and
messages about your journey,
experiencing NO DISTRACTIONS.

e-book
COLLECTION

DOWNLOAD

AUTHOR
____

Josefa Renee
www.thereneeeffect.com
info@thereneeeffect.com

Facebook: /josefarenee
Instagram: shes_outtacontrol

INFO@BAREINMINDPRODUCTIONS.COM
WWW.BAREINMINDPRODUCTIONS.COM